D0596666

THE FACE BEHIND THE FACE

The Face

LONDON · NEW YORK

Behind The Face

Yevgeny Yevtushenko

Translated by Arthur Boyars and Simon Franklin

MARION BOYARS

Republished in paperback in 1993
First Published in 1979
by Marion Boyars Publishers
24 Lacy Road, London SW15 1NL

237 East 39th Street, New York, NY 10016

Sections I–V are from *Ottsovsky Slukh* published in Moscow in 1975;
Section VI originally published as *Sneg v Tokio* in *Ogonyok* magazine in 1975.

Set in 12 pt Bodoni by Gloucester Typesetting Co Ltd,
and printed in Great Britain by
Itchen Printers, Southampton

CONTENTS

I

II

The two pictures at the front of the book are two faces of Yevgeny Yevtushenko

INTRODUCTION

The life of a poem does not begin on paper. It ends there. A poem lives – truly lives – when it is darkly palpitating within the poet, kicking around inside him, when the poet still has no clear idea of what it will become, still senses it only as a vague presentiment, a promise, a hope. A 'finished' poem – one polished to perfection – is finished, over. All poems are at their best before they are written. Hence the tragic urge to keep on writing, for the main thing is not the final full stop, but the choking torrent of commas gushing from one's gullet. All books, even the greatest, have been greater still inside their creators. Something always remains unrealized, rejecting encapsulation in words, as if there were not yet in existence words to express it all. A writer's happiness is a bitter happiness, because the joy of a labour completed is invariably laced with the hollow tang of disappointment. It is frightening to complete anything. I live in total subjection to this fear, and perhaps that is why I am sometimes so verbose, trying whatever way I can to prolong the ecstasy of incompleteness, shying away from that notorious 'compositional wholeness' and immaculately fine honing so lauded by literary bores. I have never wanted to write poems separate from one another, but rather to write something more like a novel in poems – a novel with extra instalments in which the hero can be killed

off and resurrected at will, without readers demanding it, and
even with editors objecting to it. One should read a poet not for
his individual poems, but for his books of poems. So, I despise
literary dabbling; but I detest tedium. I would always want the
reader not merely to put ticks against the poems he likes, but to
follow the author from poem to poem, as if from adventure to
adventure, constantly on tenterhooks about what will happen to
the poet next. Besides the standard Agatha Christie formulae of
crime thrillers, there are the great Dostoevskian adventures of
the human spirit, and without such great adventures there can
be no poetry.

This collection of poems is intended not simply as a collection,
but as a book, in which there is, despite the kaleidoscope of
geographical and psychological situations, a single hero. But
readers will be mistaken if they imagine that the hero of this book
is called Yevgeny Yevtushenko. I myself am, of course, that hero,
but it has never been enough for me to be merely myself. To be
truly yourself, you have to be many people. You have to look
into the mirror and be able to see not only your own face, but a
multiplicity of other faces, without which there is no you. There
is no me without the Siberian fisherman who can, with that
peculiar 'father's ear', hear by the squelching of the boots that
his son's feet are bare inside them; there is no me without that
Japanese artist, rebelling against her husband, armed defence-
lessly with paints and brushes; there is no me without Pablo
Neruda; without the lonely lampshade girl who invents some sort
of special lampshade so as to display, at least by this, her
gratitude to mankind for all its cruelty; without the malachite
frog, gazing at me with its strange, omniscient eyes. These
are not the several heroes of my book, but one and the same

hero – changing appearance from time to time, but still the same.

Man is isolated even as things are; he cannot permit himself the dangerous luxury of inner isolation. I hate the idea of forced collectivism, in which faces are erased in the name of facelessness. It is a miserable parody of what overcoming isolation really means. Isolation grows even deeper if it becomes collective. But every face has its inner face, of which we are sometimes wary, or else downright afraid. If we only stopped being frightened of revealing to each other these inner faces, we would see how close and akin to one another, how inseparable we really are. Only masks hate one another. Our faces cannot hate one another; but our faces are covered by masks. That is why this book is called *The Face Behind The Face*.

Mankind is essentially a single organism, a single body, a single soul. But can we imagine a body surviving if it were hacked into little pieces (even if in these little pieces artificial dams were to be constructed, for normal blood circulation)? Would any body withstand such bestial torture? Yet mankind endures, somehow; even hacked to pieces it somehow exists, and its separate little pieces pulsate, breathe, hope, strive to coalesce. Clearly mankind is a special kind of organism, a special kind of body and soul, possessing supernatural powers of survival. The translation of various literatures from language to language is a mysteriously powerful mutual transfusion of blood between the sliced-up pieces of the single body of mankind. Were this not so, mankind would not survive. I would like to quote the words of Thomas Wolfe, from the forty-seventh chapter of his magnificent book *You Can't Go Home Again:* 'The evils that we hate, you no less than I, cannot be overthrown with shrugs and sighs and shakings of the head, however wise. It seems to me that they but mock at us and only become more bold when we retreat before them and take refuge in the affirmation of man's tragic average. To believe that new monsters will arise as vicious as the old, to believe that the great Pandora's box of human frailty, once opened, will never show a diminution of its ugly swarm, is to help, by just that much, to make it so for ever.'

Thanks to translators for helping Thomas Wolfe to say this in Russian. Thanks to my translators for helping me to talk with you in English.

Yevgeny Yevtushenko
July 1978

I

*   *   *

You can't get away with it—
Neither the slightest detour
From your predetermined path,
Nor being friends with a scoundrel,
Nor showing off to dazzle
A fool of a star-struck girl.

You can't get away with it:
Not a false move, or a sound—
For the false has a dangerous echo—
Nor lusting for wealth,
Nor calculating steps
Up the stairs of success.

You can't get away with it—
Not the forgotten friend
Who makes you feel awkward,
Nor the tiniest ant
Under your shoe,
Squashed without spite.

This is the vicious circle:
You can't get away with it,
And even if you do,
Nothing comes free—
And a man, bit by small bit,
Goes out of his mind . . .

THE WILD ASS'S SKIN

Fear sidled into me, soft, slippery;
I feel my time is really running out.

My days were golden but my life was poor,
Time was of no particular account.

I've known restraint and freedom from restraint,
But there are still too many nuts to crack.

Quite feverishly I still scratch around,
No longer able to improve my fate.

To speak my heart comes harder all the time—
I find my nights and days are all too few.

Now I collapse exhausted on the bed—
I feel I've started more than I can finish.

I feel that as my soul strips off its rust
My words will peter out before the end.

The rustling of the wild ass's skin
Must be an omen that my soul is shrivelling.

Or is it just the thought that frightens me,
That it will shrink and disappear?

And fear dins into me: "Write, write,
Before your very soul has vanished".

HOPE

It is terrible to replace dead feelings
With memories of feelings,
But still more terrible if even
The memories are dead,
And like the spittle of black blood
You slaver onto a sheet of paper:
"Life has no meaning when it consists
Of moments made meaningless."

And with its inaudible key
Despair will enter the flat,
Like a woman, no stranger,
But somehow near and familiar.
She'll lie down beside you,
And with her cold frame will erase you,
And you'll start to feed her desire,
Yourself dwindling into a slave.

Despair is more cunning than hope
And wears the face of the wise;
But her wisdom is depraved, grasping—
She's cold and calculating.
Instead of children, warm and alive,
She'll bear you only phantoms,
And imprison time
Like a drowsy fly in amber.

As hope's wicked stepmother
She'll mock at her,
Rearrange everything—thoughts, things,
Like your legally wedded wife,
And wiping her tears with her tiny fist,
Hope will leave the house like an orphan
With a dirty bundle—
Leave the house where she is needed no longer.

She'll go out into the wide world,
She'll travel through forests and fields,
And late at night you'll wake up
In your icy lover's embrace,
Transfixed by hope's childish screams
As ruffians ravish her
In those blind alleys, where despair
Drove her into their clutches.

Search for hope, the innocent,
Like a drop of heaven in a sieve!
Search for her on every station platform,
By every precipice and bonfire!
Kill despair, the old hag!
Rescue hope in the end!
For, as Pushkin once said:
"Hope is a faithful sister".

METAMORPHOSES

Childhood is the village of Rosycheekly,
Little Silly, Clamberingoverham,
Leapfrogmorton, going towards Cruelidge,
Through Unmaliciousness and Clearvisiondon.

Youth is the village of Hopeworth,
Expansiongrove, Seducehall,
And, well, if it's a bit like Foolmouth,
All the same it is Promising.

Maturity is the village of Divideways,
Either Involvementhaven or Hidewell,
Either Cowardsbridge or Bravewater,
Either Crookedwood or Justfield.

Old age is the village of Tiredhead,
Understandmore, Little Reproach,
Forgetfast, Overgrownend,
And, God keep us from it, Lonelybury.

*　　*　　*

In moments of sudden confusion,
So as to regain your bearings
Don't demean yourself
By feeling bitter.

Don't submit
To a hateful mob.
Don't fall prey
To a lust for revenge.

"An eye for an eye,
And a tooth for a tooth . . ."
How utterly shallow!
How brainless the author!

What's all right for a cretin
In *you* is a cause for reproach.
"Holy malice"
Was Blok's[1] invention.

[1] Alexander Blok (1880–1921) Leading Russian Symbolist poet.

Be poor with dignity,
Feel calm and refreshed!
Don't gnaw at yourself!
Don't gnaw at others!

But utter forgiveness
Of all grovellers
Is dire revenge
On your friends.

And compassion
Towards all who are brutal and boorish
Is madness,
Though with a crazy logic.

Oh, how repulsive,
When one defeated
By scum
Proceeds to suck up to it.

Don't puff yourself up
Into terrible turbulence,
Don't drop down
To kiss all the arses!

WISDOM AND FOLLY

Wisdom has certainly increased
                                but folly has not deserted me.
Folly has a most amiable soul.
Folly, a very rabbit,
                        with unabating ardour,
Tries to find friends
                    in the slimy society of boa-constrictors.
Wisdom gives a wry smile:
                            "Oh, folly, get wise!
Don't look for friends in the scaly family.
You won't find any warmth in cold-snakiness.
A cold snake's
                forever a cold snake."

Folly stays cheerful:
                        "But under the scales,
I hope,
        there's something human."

Answers wisdom:
                    "Folly, I really don't know whose wife
You can be—
                    except, perhaps, an idiot's!
Now you'll tell me
                    that Myshkin was an idiot
In the reptiles' eyes,
But naive enthusiasm even in folly is no bad quality
If there's the tiniest spark of wit in it.
Give up hoping,
                    folly,
For the balm of somebody's charity,
And change the noble fire of indignation
Into lofty disdain."

I listened very closely to the argument,
Torn sometimes by pride,
                         sometimes by cowardice,
That I am master of my wisdom,
But not the master of my folly.
There's the folly of the good-for-nothing, and cattle,
There's reckless feats on precipices,
And a man is hardly a man
                         when

He's dead to the blissful folly of yielding to impulse.
What does "getting wise" really mean
When the soul sips the poison of unbelief?
Better that memory should betray me
As long as I've still got my credulity.

Wisdom,
        don't be mockingly morose;
Holy folly, don't get wise
               and worldly!
I've no respect for wisdom grown foolish,
And folly grown wise gets only my pity.

FOR YOUR ATTENTION

I wish to bring to your attention,
Passengers on this rattling train of years,
That on the map there's no sign of
                                    the destination
For which you have reserved your tickets.
It has been established with precision in the course of enquiry
That there's no
                    station
                            called Second Youth;
I wish to bring to your attention
That you dribbled away your first youth in vain,
Babies to the last,
And, regrettably, in you
                            I recognize myself.
I wish to bring to your attention
The fact that further on are the stations Old Age and Death,
But professing an unconfirmed immortality
You do not care to think of this in advance.

I wish to bring to your attention
The fact that if, gentlemen,

                    your luggage

                          contains

Perished goods

              and only the anecdotes are fresh—

Why then, you've already arrived

                    at Death station.

I wish to bring to your attention
The fact that the years, without further ado,

                           will swallow

                           you all—

Only those pale little chickens,

                  which you've gobbled up,

Will flutter like phantoms

              pursuing the train . . .

BY THE WAY

By the way,
Here's the last of my good advice:
Change back
To the boy you were once,

        let's say, at twelve.
Spring term
     is a grind
  and you want to get out to the rough-and-tumble.
Playing truant
      gives you the clean taste of a ball and freedom.
In rebelling
Against family tyranny
       and school chores
Be a new Bobrov
      shooting the ball into the rainbow!
Your satchel
Is torn,
Like its leatherette stomach was puffed out with peas,
And if it has any use—
      then it's only to stand as a goal-post.

Windows,
If they have any use—

                    it's for bashing them out with a ball.

Auntie,
If she has any use—

                  it's for scaring her with a toy pistol.

Granny,
If she has any use—

                   it's to really give her the slip.

A cap
If it has any use—

                it's for tossing it high in the air!

Through the eyes
Of a boy-into-devil,

              rebel,

                  rogue,

By your side
Suddenly dream up your

                 fortyish self.

Come on,
Scream at yourself

              out of terrible fear, out of shame:

"Uncle,
I don't want to turn into *you*,

                  not for anything, ever!"

B

WOUNDS

To D. G.

I have been wounded so often and so painfully,
Dragging my way home at the merest crawl,
Impaled not only by malicious tongues—
One can be wounded even by a petal.

And I myself have wounded—quite unwittingly—
With casual tenderness while passing by,
And later someone felt the pain,
It was like walking barefoot over ice.

So why do I step upon the ruins
Of those most near and dear to me,
I, who can be so simply and so sharply wounded
And can wound others with such deadly ease?

AN OLD FRIEND

I dream of an old friend,
                    who has become an enemy,
But in my dream he's not an enemy,
                    but still the same old friend.
He's not *with* me,
                  but he's there wherever I am,
And my head goes
                  spinning around with the dreams.
I dream of an old friend,
                    a confessional cry by the walls
On a staircase so steep
                  that the Devil would break a leg,
And his hatred,
              not of me, but of those
Who had been our enemies
                  and will remain so, thank God!
I dream of an old friend,
                  as I would of an old love
Which is already
              forever beyond recovery.

We gambled on risk,
                    we gambled on conflict,
And now we're enemies,
                    who had been two blood-brothers.
I dream of an old friend,
                    like the splashing of banners
Is dreamed of by soldiers,
                    whose war has ended in wretchedness.
Without him, I'm not "I",
                    without me, he's not "He"
And if we're enemies,
                    it's already a different age.
I dream of an old friend.
                    Like me, he's a fool.
Who's right, who's wrong,
                    I'll not begin to enquire.
What are new friends?
                    Better an old enemy.
An enemy can be new,
                    but the only friend is an old friend.

IN THE FOREST

Winter's last tiny remnants
Hardly whimper underfoot,
And the tussocks breathe as if embarrassed
By their nude defencelessness.

Along the track, adding to the rust of pine needles
Through the thawed-out grove now floats
A fragment of some child's ski,
Like a shoe with a turned-up toe.

In the forest even dirt is entirely different,
In the forest even the damp is good,
When, with foot denting the last snow,
You walk alone, never hurrying.

With me—weariness and a dog.
Suddenly the dog is lured to the side:
There, from under the snow, arose such a scent,
There, from last year, but still a bone!

As for me, I haven't been tempted for years,
Artlessly lured on by scents,
To frolic with deceptive bones
Filled only with emptiness.

The pile of my rusty illusions
Contains nothing precious to me,
And I've realized that a friend's envy
Frightens me more than an enemy's hate.

Goodbye, those who were precious,
The type for whose reprints I have
Now, in their own words, smashed
As if with a hooligan's cudgel!

The man free from spite is one of the lucky ones.
I find lamentably funny
The aggressive feebleness
Of justification-crammed correspondence.

The feeling of revenge is sterile:
"You kicked me—so I'll kick you back!"
Although we'll hardly get together again
I love and at the same time pity you.

I forgive you—without feeling wary
That you will pounce, abusing me again,
And for your own salvation's sake
I wish you would forgive me.

How good it is to be the forest's guest
And wander gently through the Spring,
Showing no interest
In self-destructive skirmishes.

And as I enter the transparent thickets,
How good it is to bite into a bud
And then discover just one line
Inside its green bitterness . . .

★   ★   ★

In verse that's worked out in advance
Lies a most delicate gravity.
This brings it repute,
And connoisseurs value it.

In verse that comes out of the air
The lightness is only too enviable;
And you can do what you like,
But *that* is poetry!

THE MOUNTAIN ROAD

To K. Gerdov

Where are we hurrying, Kostya,
We've hardly sipped the Madzhári?
We're hurrying to pay a call on the sky—
Did I hear you correctly?

In the mountains there's room for neither
Self-seeking nor anger—the sky fills everything.
But what if the sky finds us likeable
And won't let us go?

We walk, as over former domains,
Over rocks, where a spring splashes,
Over leaves, like trampling on rusty
Armour of the soldiers of Spartacus.

We walk over obsolete storms,
Over piles of forged acorns,
As over bullets frozen in mid-air,
Which once in their flight pierced people.

The man who has crammed the world's history
Into his mere mortal breast
Is forever set upright,
No one can force him to waver.

Kostya, let us think eternal thoughts
Over the fallen leaves of past years.
Let virility be light-hearted—
For there is no cunning virility.

All Jason's cunning came from servitude.
Such a lucky rogue would need no sky.
The man who's too cunning down here
Will not get to heaven.

But, without taking offence, we preferred,
As a foil to this young wine,
A simple lamb's fleece
To Colchis's fleece of gold.

There are no women truer than the road.
We three get along famously;
We're like gods of old
And lead her behind us.

The road and a pair of strong men—
A mighty triumvirate!
But beside us, in dusty sandals,
Walk Plato and Socrates!

And also, perhaps, the Three Musketeers,
And maybe even Bulgakov's cat,[1]
And he, the unforgettable,
Who walks beside all who walk.

And a crabapple very lightly
Flies into my hand, it lies there
With a ladybird, noiseless,
Upon its moist green cheek . . .

[1] A talking cat from the novel 'The Master and Margarita' by Mikhail Bulgakov (1891–1940).

THE FACE BEHIND THE FACE

Where does it live, the face behind the face?
Everyone ought
To know all that there is
About the face that is his.

People often haven't a clue
About their very own *I*.
Each of us makes his own
Best defence counsel.

Nero, apparently, thought
He was a poet,
Hitler thought that he
Would redeem the world from woe!

The mean man thinks: "I am so generous".
The shallow man: "I am profound".
Sometimes God will sigh: "I am a worm".
The worm hisses: "I am God!"

The worms climb arrogantly upwards.
The coward rejoices to be in the clouds.
Only the free man
Thinks:
> "I am a slave".

THE SOUL

There's nothing on earth more delicate
Than what is labelled 'the soul'.
Its every invisible scar
Hurts, however you soothe the pain.

But more fearful than all our fears—
Indeed, it's better kept under the knife—
Is that to shield it from shattering blows
We might cravenly buttress the soul!

The soul, a veritable watch-dog,
Tired of all the loud scuffling,
Dreams, the poor cur, even so,
Of a state where all dogs are free.

It dreams of the splendour of gutters,
Itself the soul of the town's
Dump, held back by a chain,
Though forged out of solid gold.

And if, nonetheless, it breaks free
From the chain, churning everything up,
And if, nonetheless, it meets and mates
With another soul—

                  it *proves* it's a soul!

VERBOSITY

To V. Solovyev

I am verbose both in my daily life
And in my verse—that's your bad luck—
But I am cunning: I realize
That there's no lack of will
Behind this endless drivel,
Rather my strong ill-will!

A superfluity of words conceals
Camouflaged existence's pure essence—
The thread of gold lost in the yarn.
And Vinokúrov[1], many years ago,
Speaking of the superfluous, said
It was even indispensable.

Cutting the cackle, you can't avoid dramas.
Just think, if I should stick to the point,
How crudely the message would emerge—

[1] Yevgeny Vinokurov (b. 1925) Russian poet

When like a *muzhik*, not a weakling,
I blurt it all out at once, laconic,
In good old four-letter words.

I am, thank heaven, a graphomaniac,
And one day I'll bring crashing down
Onto your heads, heavy as thunder,
A novel, 700 pages long, and more!
That's what the bard gets driven to,
That's where he'll unload his soul!

Eternal verities rest on the precise,
Precision, though, consists in sacrifice,
Not for nothing does the bard get scared—
The price of brevity is blood.
Like fear of prophecies contained in dreams,
The fear of writing down eternal words
Is the real reason for verbosity.

★   ★   ★

A drop fell
          and vanished
On that grey temple
As if it had silently buried
Itself in sand.
Are not friendship and love likewise
Interred,
Just like the body of a drop melting
On that grey hair?
Where there's a friend, then love's absence
Does not frighten us,
(Although we get the itch
From time to time.)
Absence of friends won't seem such an abyss
When love
Places its palm
As a bulwark before the precipice.
More frightening, by far, when fully-armed,
Uniting,

Both absence of love
                    and absence of friends
Encircle us.
Then we betray ourselves in mock
Depravity.
We attribute
                features of loved ones
To those not loved.
Wandering painfully,
                    as in a field,
During a blizzard,
Against our will we look for a friend
In an enemy's face.
Naive to expect a comforting word
From a dead mouth.
To demand feelings
                    is repugnant
To the very nature of feelings,
And a cold stranger
Will shrink with fear
At the frantic shriek of
"Comrade,
            friend . . ."
And a woman will sigh under her breath
From the warm shadows,
When our confessions are superfluous,

Though pretty enough.
But stuck in the glutinous morass,
And amid the losses,
One so wants to embrace somebody:
"Comrade, believe!"
And is it really a sin

                when, amid the tormented

                        gloom,

The backbiting,

            the abuse,
One so wants to say to somebody:
"I love you . . ."?

THE RINGING OF THE EARTH

A kind of ringing once dinned through my head
And right round the city of Moscow everything
Doubled, then trebled and resounded:
Tramcars, sparrows, lampposts—
And something, summoned up within me,
A pure uncoiling, went completely wild;

The ringing crashed careering down on me
As if onto a savage stallion,
And striking at my ribs with its sharp heels
The ringing called me to the sky-blue gap,
Right where the town glutted itself on pasties,
Tore everything to shreds, but in a kindly way.

The ringing knew things I didn't know myself.
It was as much at home in the pure sky
As in the trash of out-of-town ravines.
The ringing was coloured music without words,
Blending the egg-yolks of church cupolas
With red-clothed slurping splashing out of flags.

The ringing imagined verses for me
Out of rough husks of sunflower seeds
Crunched underfoot on station platforms;
And answering I rang out to the earth's ringing,
And lines rushed from the tunnel of my throat
Like railway carriages, crammed with the ringing.

And there was no more me—only the ringing.
It chose me as its incarnation,
But dropped me—started to look for someone younger.
And, as you loved me for that borrowed ringing,
You ceased to be. The ringing created you,
And you died in the ringing when it ended.

BUT BEFORE . . .

Beloved,
                can this really be you and me,
Worn out, like after illness,
By such long years of struggle,
Not with mere outsiders,
                        but with each other?
But before . . .
                Our son is crying in his sleep!
We separate . . .
                The wind is almost ripping down the house!
Come, at least once, where my eyes can follow,
Come with your former eyes.
But before we separate, as you propose,
Don't go looking for advice out there
Where the void,
                mimicking dense shrubland,
Pretends to act as wet-nurse to the moon.
But before we separate, as you propose,
Hear how the ice drones in the night,

While the bluish light transforms to green,
And that green light cuts through the dark.
But before . . .

        We lived on cruelty!
For this we deserve to be buried alive!
When did we learn to be such strangers?
When did we unlearn our way of speaking?
Her answer:

        "Don't call me 'Beloved.' "
It serves me right.

        I deserved it.

          I can say nothing.
But, by all our twisted

        broken

         life,
I beg you:

      before
You look at me,

        unseeing,
I ask you,

       and on my knees,
Calling you no longer 'Beloved':
"My old friend,

        don't leave me . . ."

*   *   *

I remember, I remember—as God's my witness—
How, being deprived of you, I almost howled;
Still, how we first met,
I forget. There's a lot I've forgotten.

Did I tremble with excitement, like a boy,
Or did the shadow which gives warning of the end
Pass like a chill of absolute knowledge
Across the pure exhaustion of my face?

Forgotten meetings bear a grudge against us,
They disappear and do not weigh us down.
And much of what I've now forgotten
Has taken vengeance by forgetting me.

I say to nothing: "Come and be reborn!"
But in my last appeal I whisper this:
"How can it be that you and I are parting
When you and I have never truly met?"

A TEAR

A tear surges up to be shed,
Surges up to be shed,
For life is complex precisely because
It ebbs away.
A tear surges up to be shed,
Surges up to be shed,
But why—

        the tongue

                cannot bring

Itself to say—
Not from insult,

        not from malice,

Not from stupidity.
A tear surges up to be shed,
Surges up to be shed,
And stops on the eyelashes
Like the tear of a fever.
A tear surges up to be shed,
Surges up to be shed,

And don't be afraid
                    that words
Are abandoned.
A tear surges up to be shed,
Surges up to be shed,
And towards where—
                    your course
Lies there concealed . . .

MOTHER

Between mother and son
                    there's a fatal lack of equality,
Especially if he's grown-up
                    and the only one.
The last man
          whose eyes a woman tries to attract,
For whom she tries to look smart—
                              is her son.
When my mother
                sits gently down on the edge
Of my bed,
              after pulling off her soaking shoes,
There rises to her lips,
                    not happy, but not reproachful either,
The question, murderously tender:
                              "Son, what's troubling you?"
You can't land an answer from a son
                              even with tenderness as bait.
Ready for
          the ground to swallow me up,

I mumble feebly:
                    "Everything's all right,
                    by the way, you're looking well . . ."
Using the false rules
                    of the cowardly son's game.
Have I really and truly nothing
                                    to say to my mother
Who's brought me up,
                    only to be ground down so helplessly?
I hide in words:
                    "Calm down . . . don't worry about anything . . ."
I *do* have things to say,
                    but I'm sorry for her—
                                    I can't speak.
The gulf between us
                    is gradually filled with tears,
But one can't bridge the gulf that makes us strangers.
Surely it's unthinkable to load
                            onto my mother's shoulders
Burdens I can hardly bear myself.
Fathers can be accidental.
                            Only mothers are always
                                        real.
No power on earth can truly replace them,

And a mother,
                coming on a visit,
                                and then going away—
Is already the sin
                of her inhuman son.
When we grow old,
                then with delayed penance
We come to our mothers,
                                to mounds of moist earth;
Then, holding nothing back,
                                we pour out
                                                to them
Everything that once,
                during their lifetimes, we could not say.

SON AND FATHER

Child, be father of the man—
After all, your father is also a child.
He'd *like* to show more authority,
But it's hard—you can tell from his face.

He's reading to you from a book
About Mowgli and Shere Khan,
But deep in himself—wound on festering wound,
He can scarcely stifle a groan.

Child, rather than turning on tears,
Cheer him up with a nice noisy game
On his way back from the jungle,
When he can't believe he's really alive.

But with your childish wilfulness
And smiling insensitivity,
Don't fool about with your inheritance—
Your father's pain!

*   *   *

Even in children there's no truth . . .

         Deceit has got to them too.

War, like a choc-ice,

        refreshes them in the cinema,

There flourishes reduced-to-scale bossiness,

         hardhearted dexterity

At pushing others away

        with their elbows by the tray.

When I notice in them

        the seeds of cruelty,

I don't, of course,

        blame them at all, not *them*,

For being young wolves

        sometimes, and not young hares,

Though, so far, they choose from

        a bloodless bill-of-fare.

An *old* toady, that's all right!

        But licking boots at five,

Sneaking at seven—

        that is what frightens me!

My son, become what you wish,

a footballer, if you like,

But at least be human!

That will solve everything.

Believe me, I've in no way

tried to slander you.

You won't understand just yet,

but when you've grown up

You'll know that only a father's fear

profanely permitted me

To tell such a lie: "Even in children there's no truth . . .".

FRESH SMELL OF LIMES

Fresh smell of limes,
A stream of bitterness,
And so for some reason
I have not succumbed.
Fresh smell of limes
All around me, hovering,
A new leaf full of resin
Stuck to my tongue,
Now a child's moan—
A ball bounced into the water.
Fresh smell of limes
Says: "Don't cry!"
An oldish chap weeps
By the beer-stall.
Take pity on him,
Fresh smell of limes!
The leaves have grown large.
With them you have saved
Me from disaster,
Chístiye Prudý.

And I'll pluck up the nerve
To be wiser than disaster
And I'll paint myself
In the benches' fresh colour.
A chess tournament
Between baldies and beards
Will make the world new:
"Your move, comrade!"
What to move, where to?
Hardly any pieces.
Read the right move
On the pond's surface.
The wind sails through
With the heat of pasties.
The wide-angle camera
Seduces one to be snapped.
Green, gold, blue,
Brightly clamorous,
The pet shop
Offers fish in jars.
Perhaps Moscow
As a Baba Yaga
Can be cuddly
Like nobody else.
God protect me,
If I have grown weak,

From not fighting back
The feeling that I'm finished.
Better to bite,
Banishing melancholy,
The taxi's bright light
Like an Antónovka apple!
Kiss in the shadow
The white arc of elbow
And draw into yourself
The fresh smell of limes.
How grudging is May—
It gives pleasure shamefully;
Don't leave it to destiny
Rather than thirst after life!
However sweet the seduction
Of living any old way may appear,
The fresh smell of limes
Can deceive!

CHISTIYE PRUDY

A couple seems to float
By the placid waters
Along the red-brown avenue
Beside Chístiye Prudý.

The world is drained of music.
It must be 3 a.m.
Like children, over-tired from running,
The voices have fallen asleep.

And silently over the water
In this quietest of Edens
This pair dances on
To its own music.

And the music hardly flows,
Gentle as silence.
It does not blare out,
But the sound is there.

And clasped by the music,
The grey street lamp feels depressed,
Like a dandelion
Which the wind is about to dismantle.

A soldier with a crew-cut
And a *Prima* in his mouth,
He seems like a little boy—
Except to himself.

The girl isn't very smart.
There's no lace on her dress,
And her Construction Brigade jacket is
Scorched through by bonfires.

On her head sits, not heavily,
Not shading her vision,
A soldier's peaked cap,
But set back-to-front.

And stroking his neck with her hand
She says rather shyly:
"Don't worry, Zhenya,
I'll be waiting for you."

And he, my gallant namesake,
Said not a word, but
Put the cap straight for her,
So that the peak faced the right way.

And with a shudder of pain,
Chewing my fag-end,
I let slip a sigh
Because it was Zhenya, but not myself.

So what do *you* mean, Yevgeny Alexandrych,
Peering into the night,
Fuming, with clouds of smoke,
Feeling bad about life?

There's a lot of evil in the world
But so much good as well,
And there's always the road
To Chístiye Prudý.

What do defeats matter, when
"Don't worry, Zhenya,
I'll be waiting for you"
Sounds so lovingly?

Dwindling talent?
What foolishness!
Can such a thought exist
Amid such things?

MEMENTO

Like a reminder of this life
Of trams, sun, sparrows,
And the flighty uncontrolledness
Of streams leaping like thermometers,
And because ducks are quacking somewhere
Above the crackling of the last, paper-thin ice,
And because children are crying bitterly
(Remember children's lives are so sweet!)
And because in the drunken, shimmering starlight
The new moon whoops it up,
And a stocking crackles a bit at the knee,
Gold in itself and tinged by the sun,
Like a reminder of life,
And because there is resin on tree trunks,
And because I was madly mistaken
In thinking that my life was over,
Like a reminder of life,—
You entered into me on stockinged feet.
You entered—neither too late nor too early—
At exactly the right time, as my very own,

And, with a smile, uprooted me
From memories, as from a grave.
And I, once again whirling among
The painted horses, gladly exchange,
For one reminder of life,
All its memories.

MALACHITE FROG

Salutations from the birch logs, small and time-worn,
That showed us such tenderness in the darkening wood
When we pressed against each other,

                                        as we sat down on them
Under the gaze of a gentle malachite frog.
Ever curling,

                the white bark of the birch
Opened slightly under my hand, so easily,
And the pulp, still pink, came seeping through
And started, so bitterly, to weep on to my hand.
Softly I stood up, rather numbed,
And went over to

                  a birch, not yet cut down,
And I pressed against its body with my own,
Rubbing my fingers

                    with chalk, like a happy schoolboy,
And the tips of my fingers

                        wiped your tears all away
With warm, powdery moth-dust

                        from that birch.

In that forest's glistening dusk
There was a constant flowing together: you into the birch,
                              the birch into you . . .
And the dusk,
                    smelling of burdock and mushrooms,
Would squeeze us again,
                         mouth to mouth within itself.
Salutations from the dusk,
                         autumnal,
                                   damp;
Don't treat the benevolent dusk
                         harshly.
Don't be afraid of it
                    when it drops in at the flat,
And give it some yoghurt to eat when it's tired,
And put it up for the night on an old camp-bed,
And ask about that
                    malachite frog.
Salutations from the skier
                         on the strangest of practice-rollers,
There on the highway,
                    in the quietest and shadiest shade,
Where sorrowing over the August asphalt
Ski-sticks would knock
                    with the lightest of sparks.

Salutations from the menacing motor car,

                                   which loomed up

Beating its way from afar with its lights through the pines,

And moved in its clumsy,

                       ponderous, oversized way,

Making all Podmoskóv'ye resound with its terrible roar,

Revolving furiously over enfeebled life

Its lightning-faced blue and white

                    rotator.

And we, as if glued to the spot,

               kept racking our brains with the question:

What kind of monster is that?

                  What distant parts is it making for?

And the car splattered us lightly with water,

And suddenly turned out to be wearing an army star

And suddenly seemed a hope—

                not a disaster,

And the soldiers' lean boyish faces

Wanted so much to share something with us . . .

And salutations from me,

             who am slightly ill,

Slightly old,

       a little ridiculous,

And drunk often,

         and sober rarely,

And foolish, luckily,
                    and wise—unluckily,
But love you very much,
                        like this August,
Like the heaviness of the air,
                            which is no burden,
Like this forest,
                where everything birch-milkily
Flows perfectly pure into everything else,
Like this car smelling of young life,
With a wet army star,
Like a freckle dropped into the dirt by a skier,
Like the gentle malachite frog.

IRON STAIRCASE

In the entrance to your block of flats on the Petróvka
There's an iron staircase.
Its pre-revolutionary pattern
Is worn to a gun-metal blue.
The boots of the swells in gaiters
Used to scuff the steps,
And tattered vixens, baring their teeth,
Used to leer from the shoulders of whores.

Here felt boots, leggings
And overshoes used to compete,
Initialled galoshes,
And boots of the Secret Police.
Also such gutter talk as:
"Gimme the dough, Mister!"
Then the more ladylike "Really, Kitten!"
And the totally proletarian
"Bugger off!"

On this very staircase, perhaps,
Rasputin threw up
And Savinkov offered a cold Browning
Automatic to a girl student;
And I will visit you at midnight,
And my ringing will wake
You—who have as many secrets
As Moscow itself.

And you won't be surprised to see me, as if
We'd arranged a secret rendezvous,
And you'll understand everything, without my explaining,
Without any need to be taught;
You, there, warm as a raisin-roll in the morning
Straight from the baker's,
With raisin moles on your neck,
With gleaming raisins for eyes.

You, like Moscow, are all hidden in Moscow,
You, a number in the street directory,
Hide, like a house which
Has not yet been completely gutted—
Only sometimes does your gaze glitter
Icily, like a Maximalist,
Whose chances today of being herself
Would be minimal!

In the entrance to your block of flats on the Petróvka
There's an iron staircase
Which we tread at different times,
But in one and the same crowd
As all of you, dear
And repellent ghosts:
Where, gradually, we ourselves will
Turn into ghosts . . .

THE EASTER PROCESSION

There was a procession at the church in the suburbs:
The priest swinging his Vesuvius-on-a-chain,
And a crowd of old women with candles in their hands.
The old age pensioners, hardly able to stand,
Lifted their banners with a hymn of faith,
And Christ's Image swayed unsteady in the clouds.

In *Vólgas, Zhigulís* and *Zaporózhets's*
The crowds rolled up—congestion on the route to Christ!
They belched and shoved their neighbours black and blue.
Then the pawing started, an extra bit of fun,
Like at a match, where, just for a lark,
They play football with the head of Christ.

Midget Man's essence was revealed again:
To get himself a better inch of space.
What's gained in scrapping is the Lord's own gift!
And so the vespers was their battlefield—
For these lads, mini-Beatles, it's all the same,
Jesus Christ or Adamo.

Two rather quiet and clearly highbrow girls
Attached themselves to the old women in the crowd,
Sidling along like proper democrats.
Hiding behind a wall of Part-Time Constables,
With faces of repulsive bureaucrats,
The mob of priests stepped out with pomp.

There was a whiff of port and incense mixed with sweat,
The kind of smell you get in sour, stale marshland
Where the snipe won't even try to whistle.
Forgive me, Christ, for my hard-hearted question:
But was it ever worth your sacrifice
To stick your image in such vulgar shows?

But how is that old woman guilty of vulgarity,
Terrorized by all the flurrying
And turmoil of the drunk, rampaging crowd?
Her hand, so overworked with upraised candle,
Like a grandmother straining towards her kidnapped
      grandson,
She, Christ, so stretches out to you.

When the flock went back into the church,
The door squeezed out the overflow like toothpaste,
And there rang out a cry, shrill through a hundred yards!

The door so pressed on the old woman's hand
That only the first joint of her poor fingers
Entered the building, reaching out to Christ.

Crucifix—you are like a crossroads:
One end in fire,
                        the other in depravity.
But you, Christ, also accept
                        this world.
Do not permit that for the simple souls
All should begin in a mirage of miracles,
And end with bolted doors.

*   *   *

So who, in hell's name, are you,
What's so special about *your* fate,
That you fall over, lapping up vodka,
And still give yourself such airs?

So who, in hell's name, are you,
When, like absolute riff-raff
Glinting with plastic ear-clips,
You've started playing the Golden Girl.

So who, in hell's name, are you,
Acting the slave to dubious praise,
You coward, stopping up the mouths
Of those who still had any faith in you?

So who, in hell's name, are you,
And who, in hell's name, am I,
That I can howl, reproaching you,
Still bound to you with chains of longing?

*   *   *

Why didn't you understand me,
You demanding conscience of mine?
It was only lack of strength undermined me,
Having set me against you!

Why didn't you understand me
When you scornfully squared the accounts?
It was not being dead to your claims
That made me so weak, it was tiredness!

Why didn't you understand me?
But perhaps I didn't understand *you*,
When I gave you my hand
And you didn't give yours in return.

But you understood perfectly
That excessive heat was drawing us
To the fatal blurring of that line
Which divides good from evil . . .

POTATO FLOWER

Impertinent,
        but no blasphemer,
I love, as god's gift, asphodel
And lily-of-the-valley,
             and the cornflower
But I detest any catspiss-guttery
Flowery-scented *Eau-de-Cologne*,
Corrupting the chaste odour
Like chemical verses.
And better than any—
          joking aside—
I love the flower of the simple potato,
As I love my brother,
For its smell of earth untainted with caramel,
For the fact that no one could possibly devise
A deception
       at least out of *it*!

*   *   *

When I cast off for the canopy of ages
I should like to rest in the open air,
Not in a rainbowed Garden of Eden,
But in a plain vegetable patch!

So that all around my face
Life might guiltily grow green
With pimples of a cucumber,
With its faintly bluish bloom.

And that against my teeth might scrape,
Springing nimbly into my lips,
A beautiful delicate carrot,
With earth in its youthful wrinkles.

And that a cheeky little shoot,
Alarmingly precocious,
Might spike me in the side, indecently:
"Move up! You're stunting my growth!"
And I would ask him:

                         "Comrade,
Who are you—
                  an onion or a garlic?"

II

★   ★   ★

Once people
            get under
                        my skin,
They never find the exit.
They romp around,
                        fill my insides with their song and dance
Make lots of noise, using my dumbness as their cover-up.
I'm full to bursting
                        with wise men
And fools—
                        they've utterly exhausted me!
So much so that my skin's
                                    quite worn through
By their heels, rubbing from inside!
Give me a chance to breathe!
It's all impossible!
                        I'm stuffed to the gills
With those who've brought me so much joy
As well as those who've given most offence.
What has come over me?

What can I do with this great throng
Stuck in my own small heart—
Police are needed to keep order there!
I've gone a little cracked,
For there, in that secluded shade,
I've dropped none of the women
And none of them's dropped me!
It's awkward to revive dead friendships
However much you tire yourself with trying.
The only friends I've lost
                    were on the outside,
But of those inside I've lost nobody.
All the people in my life I've quarrelled with,
                              or made friends with
Or only shaken hands with,
Have merged in a new life under the old one's skin—
A secret conflagration without flame.
The repossession of the unpossessable
Is like a waterfall that rushes upwards.
Those who have died
                    have been born again in me,
Those who have not been born as yet
                              cry out.
My population is too large,
Beyond the strength of just one man—
But then, a person would be incomplete
If he contained no others.

A FATHER'S EAR

To M. & Yu. Kolokol'tsov

The foot-cloths had already dried over the bonfire
And two fishermen were listening to the waters of the
Vilyúi;[1]
One was, I imagine, over fifty,
While the other was
still too young to own a passport.
The father brushed the breadcrumbs
From his stubble into his palm,
Then washed them down with fish soup,
thick as honey.
A tooth—
gold, as it happened—
Clapped against the blackened aluminium of the spoon.
The father was leaden-faced with fatigue.
On his forehead, as if in layers, receded
War,
work,
employment without end
And apprehension for his son—
the father's secret cross.

[1] Siberian river

Rummaging for a tear in the net,
The father said,
                    thrusting his hand towards the sun:
"Mishka, just you take a look,
                    the mist
Is clearing after all . . .
                    It's beautiful!"
The son went on eating with a show of scorn.
A white-gold forelock hid his eyes
With such a haughty overhang of hair
As if to say why should I raise my head for such a trifle.
Then he flicked a fish-eye from his sailor's shirt
And pulled his fishing boots right on,
With their billowing turn-downs, proof of the luxury
Of this life
                    where people know their way around.
The father stamped out the smoking bonfire
And muttered as if completely by the by:
"I can hear from your boots, Mishka,
You've left your foot-cloths off again . . ."
The son responded with a youthful blush
Betraying his humiliation.
Pulling off his fishing boots,
                    he pushed his feet into foot-cloths,
Then angrily rammed them back into his boots.

But even *he* will understand—

                            too late, it's true,
The isolation of our spirit and our flesh
When there is nobody on earth who hears
The things heard by a father's ear . . .

LAMENT FOR A BROTHER

With blood still dripping from its
                              warm and sticky beak,
Its neck dangling over a bucket's edge,
A goose lies rocking in a boat,
                              like an ingot
Of slightly tarnished silver.
There had been two of them flying above the Vilyúi.
The first had been brought down in flight
                              while the other,
Gliding low,
              risking his neck,
Hovers over the lake,
                      cries over the forest:
"My dove-grey brother,
                        we came into the world
Clamorously breaking through our shells,
But every morning
                  mother and father
Fed you first,
              when it might have been me.

My dove-grey brother,
>>> you had this blue
>>>>>> tinge,
Teasing the sky with a bold similarity.
I was darker,
>>> and the females desired
You more,
>>> when it might have been me.
My dove-grey brother,
>>>>>> without fear for the return,
You and I flew away, over the seas,
But obnoxious geese from other lands surrounded
You first,
>>> when it might have been me.
My dove-grey brother,
>>>>>> we were beaten and bowed.
Together we were lashed by the tempests,
But for some reason the water slid
More easily off *your* goose's back,
>>>>>> when it might have been mine.
My dove-grey brother,
>>> we frayed our feathers.
People will eat both of us by the fireside—
Perhaps because the struggle to be first
Devoured you,
>>> consumed me.

D

My dove-grey brother,

        half our lives was a pecking match,

Not treasuring our brotherhood, our wings and our souls.

Was reliance really impossible—

I on you,

      and you on me?

My dove-grey brother,

        I beg at least for a pellet,

Curbing my envy too late;

But for my punishment people killed

You first,

     when it might have been me . . ."

SOMEWHERE ABOVE THE VITIM[1]

To E. Zommer

Somewhere above the Vitím,
Delicately gilded
By the moon, rocked from within,
A friend and I walked side by side,
Sometimes through forest, sometimes through meadow,
When suddenly we froze before a wooden hut.

That structure was quite luminous
As if it had been built
Not out of logs, but out of moonbeams.
Its very skin was resinous,
And with, as yet, no people and no cats,
The wooden hut belonged to nobody.

We entered it unfinished as it was,
And totally trusting. At its will,
Wind whistled through its wooden joints.

[1] Siberian river

The floor was rough and bare
And in the frames, instead of glass,
The Milky Way was cut out into squares.

In curls of fresh-planed wood
A pair of friendly mugs
Slept, as if embracing, on the floor.
A tool, left by the carpenters,
Tasteful and sensible,
Surveyed the newcomers from its corner.

The hut boasted no icon
But the roofing fashioned
Laws of its own, it didn't leak.
There was a cricket singing in the straw,
And Russia resided in that house
Despite the absence of its tenants.

Despatched from worlds above,
Families of future mice,
Or rushes, possibly, were audible.
As lullabies for sorrows,
Future clocks on the wall
Ticked slowly in the silence.

It was so quiet and calm!
The listener could even hear
The mushrooms growing steadily.
And dozing was rather like going
On a kind of flight within the lonely
Cosmos of the wooden hut.

Still in our sailor's shirts,
We stretched ourselves, twin-fashion.
On the floor and smoked a while.
It seemed ingenious that the hut
Was being fitted with its bridal crown—
Over an already twin-filled belly.

And in the morning this increased
To four of us, all in the world,
Because the carpenters arrived.
With unrestrained brief brotherhood
We gurgled, swallowing some milk,
Drinking a toast to Mother Earth.

Once more above the Vitím,
Now gilded by the sun,
We walked through the tiger lilies

Slightly tipsy on milk.
The sound of the carpenters' planes
Was our distant accompaniment.

In those days we were young,
And milk was like wine.
In the light a delicate
Wood shaving continued to quiver—
A light-brown companion
On my open collar . . .

LAMPSHADES

To V. Toporygin

The names of the towns have such a curious ring
Like something totally outlandish,
There, in the lampshade workshop
                              serving trains
Excitingly long-distance.
Lampshade girls
                    old and young;
Lampshades
            green and gold.
One must fashion the frame,
                              and carelessly won't do!
And then bind the disciplined wire
With unruly viscose,
So that it lies nice and even.
If one should get an international order,
Then somebody's executive eye appears;
It persistently hints, from behind one's back,
Screwing itself up majestically,
At the importance of lampshades
For the country's prestige.

And
          having fought all his wars long ago,
                              having used up his daring,
An invalid sits there—
                    Head of the Lampshade Department
And fusses over a not-so-old
Lampshade girl, Varvara,
Who's kind, as a rule,
                    mad about her work,
But with Baba Yaga's nature,
A loner,
        a smoker,
                a drinker,
Gets up on the wrong side
Almost every morning.
Her first husband was killed at Budapest
In '45,
        aged twenty-two.
At nineteen,
            stunned,
She emerged a widow.
Her second husband was jealous,
                        a nervous type—
Wouldn't forgive her for grieving over the first.
Her third husband got drowned while drunk.
And Varvara was on her own.

The 'Head' had been a bachelor for years,

                        a proper stay-at-home.

He was full of his lampshade victories

And lampshade defeats;

In the past eight years he had proposed

Eight times to Varvara.

She had always refused . . .

                    Tormenting himself,

And to celebrate his hard-earned kopeks,

He invited Varvara

To *Kalína Krásnaya* that evening.

She enjoys the film,

               but it's depressing,

She almost cries,

               clutching her handbag.

Better, after all, Indian films,

Where there's singing,

                 where it's bright and warm.

Also be thankful for comedies:

Not truthful,

              but pretty, all the same.

There's enough bitter truth in real life,

So why have it in books

                or at the cinema!

She has a hostile view of those who pity her:

"Just leave my soul alone!

Wipe the floor with me, if you like,
Only don't call me a rag!"
Well, and after the cinema—

                the restaurant

Yuzhnyi.
The tables have lampshades,
Good ones.

          One could learn something.
Smoothing the cloth with her hand,
She shyly asks
The Head Waiter:

            "Where's it from?"
He answers:

          "From Hungary . . ."
In the morning,

            after a sleepless night,
She hands the 'Head' a rough sketch,
Not copying, incidentally,
That Hungarian lampshade at all,
But breaking some special ground
In lampshade affairs.
Her face darkens,

            she looks like death.
She bends gloomily over her work,
But if she suddenly smiles
Then young girls can't match her looks.

BELATED NURSEMAIDS

I regret and yet I don't regret
That I'm in hospital and that I'm ill,
It's useful to be ill sometimes.
Hospital protects, brings comfort.
Hospital quietens murmurs in the heart
With the sighing slippers of the nurses.

On the ploughed field of death are Russian peasant girls,
They drag the bed-pans, jars and phials,
And clean up blood and vomit;
This lack of squeamishness revives
Everything within us which we really felt
Had quite decayed and could not be revived.

In hospitals our natures undergo conversion.
The nurses teach us to be kind to people.
Struggle had made us too embittered.
For us war was a callous nurse.
This age has not exactly nursed us gently,
Nor have we nursed ourselves with care.

But yet, in hospital, if we are feeling poorly,
We hear the lullaby of nurse's apron,
Rustling oh so quietly in the corner;
And a white fragment of a button
From a nurse's apron, piercing the darkness,
Shines on the floor like the star of Russia.

So soft, the curd-like colour of the nurses' kerchiefs.
The careful rustle of their moistened rags
Expunges from the sick their bounds of age.
Invisible childhood surely lurks in us,
And late, too late, the hospitals award us,
As we approach old age, our earliest nursemaids.

FOR THOSE IN PAIN
To Dr. T. P. Skvortsóva

The sailors' toast: "For those at sea;"
The geologists': "For those in the field!"
Mine, in a hospital corridor,
Is a whispered: "For those in pain . . ."

Wander around in any hospital
Invisible, in a magic white coat,
Take a look at mankind's faces
And humanity's photographs.

Take a look at the cardiograms:
Humanity's dramas are found there,
And take a look at the tests:
There are the tangled threads of fate.

Be healthy to your heart's content,
But let the hospital remind you of pain
And let the result of your blood-test
Show that you are not cold-blooded.

As you enter the screaming white gloom,
Don't let your stomach turn over,
Hear the pericardial sacs crackle
Like overstrained shopping nets.

Ghastlier than the ghastliest prose
Are tuberculosis and brucellosis.
In men's and women's live bodies
Damnable pincers are grating.

Let us forget battle for ever
And freely devote all we've got
To only one kind of armament—
Armament against pain!

So as to give Russia a shock,
You may request from mankind
Not just a temporary anaesthetic
But permanent salvation.

HEART MURMURS

Not disabled, though I can't last for ever,
I caught—my own worst enemy—
An inflammation of the membrane round the heart,
Or, to put it learnedly, pericarditis.

Heart murmurs—not a frightening diagnosis;
I'll lie down a bit, rest in the quiet,
And in fact the hospital's no problem,
I'd say it was more of a relief.

And I, given the soul of one who's able
To run himself to ruin, like a race horse,
Kept on ceaselessly murmuring, till I murmured myself out.
In my heart there was this murmur: all around me—silence.

My heart, don't go on murmuring in vain,
Don't be ill for no earthly reason.
You and I have campaigned with distinction
Through many an escapade and battle.

My heart, don't murmur like the wind,
Don't murmur like a squeaky lift,
Or like an invalid who petulantly murmurs
At station buffets, when it's closing-time.

I wore you down myself, just like a grater,
I myself brought on your stabbing pain,
But you are no silent calf or heifer,
You murmur, and that's because you're mine!

Here they've injected me with something fiery
From a syringe, and banishing hospital thoughts,
I don't want them to transplant into me
Somebody else's dull, respectful heart.

MEMORY'S REVENGE

It would appear, then,
                    that it's impossible
For me ever to be reconciled with my memory.

It and I have long been at daggers drawn.
Having jostled me onto a dark track,
Knocking me over,
                    then sticking its knee in my chest,
It holds a knife to my throat:
"So you loved someone, did you?
                              And what did you do
To love,
        stabbing it like that below the heart?"—
"I didn't mean . . ."
                    Then, to me, out of the dark:
"Accidentally?
            Ha ha . . .
                        How very kind!
I'll spare you,
            you won't die,

But I'll pierce you,
                    pay you a knife for a knife!
As a knife
            in your body I'll remain
                              living with you
All your life—
            that's how your memory takes its revenge!"

I've no need to remember you—
For under my shirt, straining at the nylon
As it sticks out of my ribs,
                        a knife-handle breathes
Bandaged with adhesive tape . . .

PAUSE

To Yu. D.

When time announces a pause,
Let a warlike throbbing arouse us,
Not a coward's throbbing, throb of reverse,
But a joyful throbbing, spearheading the attack.

It's bravery's right, with a cry
Wrenched out in the charge, to become history.
A dawn arrives, humility set aside,
Which heralds time's birth out of timeless wastes.

Everything falls to bits when that damned bitch
Pause, the glutton, gulps us all down.
Guileless, with crystal courage,
Boys, create some action in the interval!

Make sure you're in time—
Don't give in to chaos! Strike,
Storming the pause!
Storming the pause!

IN THE STUDENTS' READING ROOM

In the students' reading room,

                        splattering of pages

Like the splattering not of a storm,

                        but of the prelude to a storm.

In the lowered,

              youthful

                    serious faces

I see the flickering

                of *your* face,

                      history!

Students of Russia,

                I greet you!

Students,

            match the greatness of your Motherland!

I want you to transform the country,

Filled with the country's history,

As with the light hum of one of Pushkin's stanzas.

Ship of Peter,

              sail on, temple of learning!

Let books not splinter from the lofty masts

And let them turn, there, next to the sky,
Into crystal captains of revolution!
Let orations shatter the air with sudden thunder,
And a new Mayakovsky emerge for you!

Now the people's heart
                              is the flower of society
And not a phoney foreign *beau monde*.
Now you're not one of the intelligentsia
                                             unless you have
Guts, like a worker,
                        wisdom, like a peasant.

Students,
             you are the realm of my hopes.
Let love of freedom, maturing year by year,
Never flow over into shameful freedom
From our people.

May you,
             not curbing your headstrong natures,
Rise above times of seduction,
And never turn into those
Whom once you despised.

I don't want to play the professor.

I

Hope
        that a bench may also be found for me,
So as always to study with you,
As a carefree perpetual student.
In the students' reading room,

                        in the new world,
I hope
        that I shall remain at least a word—
That word
                which echoed in the distance—
And rustle once again in students' hands;
The page marked by a comb,

                        some of whose teeth are broken
By the unruliness of youthful hair . . .

THE SIGNPOST: 'TO YESENIN'[1]

To V. Sokolov

In the Vagán'kovskoye cemetery timid April
Pipes through its thawed-out reed.
Even the crosses smell, a little bashfully, of Spring;
Black earth is sold by weight at stalls,
And Russian soil is brought to the deceased for judgement
In damp containers made of cellophane.
Somebody's fingers press seeds into the earth.
Somebody's lips grow pale from whispering names,
And softly through the crosses and signs of Spring beckons
The signpost: 'To Yesenin', nailed onto a pine.

The caretakers, old crones, clutching the handles
Of their spades, burn faded paper wreaths,
And survey all mortalities and immortalities,
Re-silvering the tips of rusty fences.
In every Russian, above his pains and his indignities,
Is firmly nailed a signpost: 'To Yesenin',
And through the slightly acrid smoke the people come
Not to Yesenin's grave, but straight to *him*.

[1] Sergei Yesenin (1895–1925)—referred to by Gorky as "The greatest lyrical genius since Pushkin". The peasant poet *par excellence*.

Here are no paper flowers, no nylon blooms;
The people understand, *he* was no paper poet!
Here comes a taxi-driver, cap in hand;
After a sleepless night his face is grey, unshaven,
But from his heavy hand blossoms the whitest rose-bud
Like a sigh, lighter than any puff of smoke.
A bookkeeper is opening his worn briefcase
And from it he plucks April, soft as down:

Pussy Willow catkins—flowers by another name!—
His eyes are steeped in peasant melancholy.
A retired jockey retrieves some gladioli
From a crumpled copy of 'Futból-Khokkéy,'[1]
And a minuscule cadet from the Academy
Adds an Egyptian flower shaped like a bird.
A girl student carries a small potted cactus . . .
Rushes and sonchus would be appropriate here,
Goose-foot and wormwood are a perfect choice,
And for those Ryazani eyes, the blue of camomile . . .

They read his verses—far from any stage;
A boy—his forelock hides his brow like lumpish anthracite,
But in his pupils, dark as the cloudy day,
Yesenin's sky-blue firmament shines through.

[1] A weekly newspaper devoted to football and ice-hockey.

Here an old woman reads, visiting the graveyard,
A fish's tail pokes out of her shopping-bag,
But all the same, with one uncluttered hand,
She follows every line in the young air . . .

What did that little imp give Russians as a bribe?
The fact he gave *no* bribes and wasn't bribed himself.
The signpost: 'To Yesenin' points like an arrow
To the place where goodness and integrity survive.
The signpost: 'To Yesenin' points like an arrow
To where Russia was yesterday, is now, and will be always.

How is he not sublime, who deceived no people
With a false Christ, but relieved their lives a little?

TO THE MEMORY OF SHUKSHIN[1]

In art it's cosy
                    to be a fancy French brioche,
But that way you'll not properly feed
                        either widows
                            or cripples
                                or orphans.
Shukshín was the crusty end of a loaf
                        with a red guelder rose[2] as a sweetener,
That slab of black bread
                        without which the people cannot exist.
They walked in crowds to the coffin,
                            almost from Tishinsky Market.
The air, quickened by breathing,
                                quivered almost audibly.
Like a congealed drop of blood
                        of Russia herself,

[1] Vasilii Shukshín (1929–1974)—Russian film actor and director, prose-writer and author of screen plays.

[2] In Russian 'Kalína Krásnaya'—title of film starred in, written and directed by Shukshín.

Covered in red guelder roses,
                            lay the Russian artist.
When we have risen
                    on heavy peasant yeast,
We are attracted to nature,
                       to Yesenin's pure verses.
We can't get accustomed to lies,
           we can't feel at home in the grass-snake's snuggery,[3]
And the heart's like the falcon,[3]
                    like the bound Stepan Razin.
Art belongs to the people
                when it's not spoiled by the sugar of deceit,
But when it's been salted through and through
                  with the salt of its native soil.
... Shukshín's dream
                of Stepan's role, unrealized,
Like the Volga, swelled up for a moment
                beneath the ice of frozen eyelids.

[3] Reference to Maxim Gorky's 'Song of the Falcon'.

POET AT THE MARKET

At the Cheryómushkinsky market a poet
Queued
                for honey,
And a jar,
                removed from the basket,
Shone none-too-happily in her hands.
The poet was thin and grey
And her minute form seemed barely whole,
As if time,
                while chewing her to shreds,
Had suddenly coughed her up
Before the final gulp.
The poet was once famous
For a poem which sizzled with burning huts and tanks,
But the glow of those flames
                                cast no
Reddish reflection on the half-litre jar.
She stood unrecognized.
                        A market . . .

People didn't know the fate of her two loved ones.
They didn't know whom the poet had
Been up against
                and proved her courage.
Nobody knew,
                among the cabbage and fat,
That even nearing sixty,
                      forgotten by all,
The poet was now writing better than ever.
Nobody knew.
                Ignorant times!
Long ago the poet had two daughters:
One dashed off to marriage
                far away;
The other lay dying.
                  The doctor had a notion
That she needed honey—
                pure and natural.
The poet queued in silence,
                but unbowed.
One could sense in her,
                framed in pure light,
The mournful pride found
In a woman
              and a Russian poet.

She told me all about her daughters.
There were no tears.

               I only imagined them.

I offered her a lift.

               It had begun to rain.

The poet reflected a moment

               and refused.

AN ARTIST

I revere you
When you put on an act
Of completely and utterly not loving me,
And with your childlike brow all screwed-up,
In your hard little sketch book
You scratch out some foul little drawings.

Eyes made-up,
A slight hint of grey
Cultivated in your dark hair.
You say rather spitefully,
That you've been unlucky,
But you don't feel any self-pity.

You enter the Metro
Like a girlish Pierrot,
Or like Mary Pickford with her tiny pistol.
The gun's so angry with everyone,
Tucked away in your little handbag,
With its aim to get even with the whole wide little world.

E

You should be starring
On the silent screen together
With splendid Douglas Fairbankses!
But in talkies there are words,
And their essence is dead for you.
It's been years since you trusted in words.

When, in your denim jacket,
You step into the Moscow streets,
Tripping daintily out of the front door,
There's no dandified hand
From a former age
To toss you a fur coat.

You need a chorus of gypsies,
A highwayman lover,
Or the kind of smart coachman who'll send your heart
leaping.

Yours are tearaway drawings
Resembling *Scrolls*
By the once-young Zabolótsky.[1]

[1] Nikolai Zabolotsky (1903–1958). His 'Scrolls'—a collection of poems published in 1929—satirized Leningrad life in the period of the New Economic Policy.

I revere you
Like a living legend
Of the N.E.P. years,
                    gloomy,
                            sordid;
And if you are kind
I'll ask you for love
As if asking for love from the past.

A REMARKABLE MONUMENT

At the foot of the ridge of Gagry
There's a remarkable monument,
A gravestone,
                    unfurled like a sail,
Striking panic in the cemetery.
Its colour is severely funereal,
                              but it shows no trace of grief,
Because in this stone's modest artistry
Are sung the praises
                    of the just over twenty year old
Zakaryán Arutyún Amazáspovich.
He was, it seems, converted into marble
                              from a photograph.
He stands white-toothed
                    smiling,
And the white-toothed accordion
                              in his hands
Smiles too,
          as one would expect.

Above a curly forelock

                      a roomy Caucasian cap

Is delightfully

              tilted sideways,

And with live silver,

                   Arutyún Amazáspovich is washed

To the tune of the rumbling thunder!

The inscription suits him:

                 'To son, husband, father . . .'

He plays saucily,

            rocking.

Even being a father need not prevent one

                     from being a lively young fellow,

So that even after the end

                the end's still far off.

The relatives wailed

             as they buried him;

On his tombstone they wrote:

                 'He perished tragically . . .'

But at his feet lie persimmons,

               a free gift on the path,

And Egyptian beer, already opened.

The reckoning with life is settled,

                  but it's a great honour

After death

        to retain your identity.

The mist floats downwards—
                    attracted to people.
A whiff of eternity,
                    a whiff of antiquity.
Arutyún Amazáspovich,
                    you enjoy company,
Hammer the instrument with your fingers,
                    raise your head higher,
Make the sounds beat down like hail,
                    so that the tin graveyard doves
Flutter up from the fences!
Nobleman, peasant—
                    I see no distinction,
Because peasant keys play
To the surge of the sea
                    and to all the doves,
(Not forgetting the ones made of tin
                    in the graveyard).
The man who relates
                    to the real world,
Not a world of monkish isolation
                    is not going to die.
We'll be meeting again
                    and we'll sample the persimmons,
Zakaryán Arutyún Amazáspovich!

*   *   *

Lack of content is when a person's too cowardly
To bend his back under the weight of the age.
As for me, I prefer awkwardness, heaviness,
Even overloadedness at least with *something*!

Lack of content is smug self-satisfaction.
It's disgusting to sweeten another's pain;
And sugar sprinkled onto screaming wounds
Causes, perhaps, a sharper pain than salt.

TO BEGINNERS

A distressingly businesslike spirit
Glimmers
        in certain beginners.
A depressingly 'smooth' look
To lines
        which haven't known the torture
                of rough drafts.
In ever-so-neat verse making,
Where the happy ending comes with a flourish,
Having no character
        has become its character,
And having no face
        is the face!
I implore
        as desperate daring,
The skill to be clumsy!
I implore,
        as an act of courage,
Just one genuine word!

How to write
> and what about—save your enquiries.

Ask life,
> and leave it at that!

Poetic fearlessness
Is fear when the page stares back at you, empty.
How to define the creative mood
I couldn't care less.
> I'll tell a small secret:

It's in bridging the gap
Between the word
> and our hearts.

Don't expect an apotheosis,
But a mixed blessing is
The state
> of *not* being in a state

To betray
> by your words
>> the truths which lie under them.

Whose side are you on, turbulent youth:
>> the snow-swept night

Or the essential recommendation
For the long hoped-for writers' paradise?

Whose side are you on:

the Master[1]

or Woland?

Whose side are you on:

hunger

or the fat of the land?

Choose!

[1] From Bulgakov's 'The Master and Margarita', see note to page 29

IV

BE A MAN

In the harsh request
                    "Be a man!"
Made by a friend
                    or a wife,
Have you really not read the answer
To how we should
                    live?
Take a look
At the world's inhumanity:
There, crouched over the atom button,
                                        a micro-
Organism.
Under the bacterial signs of swastikas
And other malicious insignia,
A tadpole once again
Inspires
            some amoebas.
It's frightening if you,
                    my contemporary,

In a world of bullets
                    and bombs,
Still walk on all fours,
Though you've certainly sat
                    behind the wheel.
Mother cooks
            and washes for her son—
A useless honour:
Through the nylon shirt
Peeps the fur of *pithecanthropus*.
Out of the debauches
                    the drunkenness
                            the obscenities,
The very protoplasm of concentration camps,
Bestiality crawls
            sullen
                shaggy—
Unworthy even of the beast.
Bestiality strides
            its tusks unbared—
It's so refined!
TV in an electronic cave:
That's its surrogate window.
Smoke is wafted on the sorrowful wind.
Smoke from the holocausts whispers to us:
"One isn't born human,

One becomes it!"
And yearning for man are
The thinning forest,

                    black snow,

Poisoned rain,

              dead rivers,

And even man himself . . .

KOMPROMISE KOMPROMISOVICH

Kompromise Kompromisovich
Whispers to me from within:
"Come on, no need to be temperamental,
Alter the line just a little!"
Kompromise Kompromisovich
Is no fanatical hangman.
In the guise of a friend,
                              thinking grand thoughts,
He pushes us nearer the top.
He encourages drinking (in moderation),
Even a little debauchery,
Sinners are worth his while:
A bit of sin makes a man
                              a bit of a coward.
Counting it all up on the abacus,
Kompromise, the Recruiter,
Buys
     us like big
Babies, with trinkets.
He buys us with flats,

Bits of furniture,

        togs,

And we drop our hectoring tone,

But we get fairly rowdy—

              if we drink.

Something—

       listen carefully—

               clicks

In the ZIL fridge.

Kompromise, with his little rosy cheeks,

Has just sunk his white teeth in the salmon.

Hardly as

       large as a gnome,

That little tramp Kompromise

Sometimes

       sticks out his

Tongue at us from the TV.

The *Zhigulí* has just been bought,

And there's that cunning rogue Kompromise

Swinging from a string

Like a free baby doll!

Kompromise Kompromisovich

Is superb as a writer—

The author

       of heart-rending

Savings books.

Kompromise Kompromisovich,
'Our friend'
            weighed down by his duties,
Who, because he's a
                  soft and polite little rat,
Bit by bit eats us up . . .

POMPEII

Man falls apart,
             sheds his wits,
If his strength
             of mind
                    grows feeble.
Man perishes
             like Pompeii,
Bringing down
             Vesuvius
                    upon himself.
Eagerness for power
             or vulgar glory
Has turned his head,
             has led him by the nose,
But in the underground cauldron
                    the lava's already simmering,
The lava
       which
             people themselves have cooked up.

Lava doesn't spare

        temples

           or pedestals,

And it rushes in,

        without ringing the bell,

Making moulds out of people,

           as it finds them,

Burning their flesh,

        preserving their postures.

What will the bankrupt spirit bequeath?

              Moulds of indolence,

Moulds of slavery,

        moulds of shameless conceit,

Moulds of orgies,

        of business-like copulations,

And inside all these moulds—

        nothing!

Man has an urge to buck himself up with blarney,

He bathes in the bootlicking, burbles buckets,

Revels in luxury,

        like a Roman swell in a marble bathhouse,

While the volcano

        is already smoking over his shoulder.

He sits there

        pissed as a newt,

He's forgotten
                    he gave up being human long ago;
He's forgotten
                    why Pompeii was punished—
And amnesia is always
                            the start of the trouble.
How the bubbles play inside the goblet!
But in the Pompeii of the tavern
                                    the black dust
Of the vexed volcano
                    has already settled
On the crucified barbecued chicken . . .

A CHILDISH SCREAM

An exasperating childish scream,
Loud enough to set off a nervous spasm
Among the lovers of a peaceful hour,
Forced its rebellious way into Parnassus,
And the cup of patience, so to speak,
Of all makers of books really ran over.

Shields won't protect you in the least.
There's something crawling, something squealing
Under the very feet of realism.
The childish slogan screams: "War on the creators!"
How unlike your cold, efficient fathers,
Children, it seems you've really broken from your chains!

That snub-nosed youngster is quite vicious.
He keeps on blowing a policeman's whistle
So that his daddy's novel won't work out.
And virtuosically hopping on one leg,
The daughter of the critic G. is throwing
Cherry stones into his 'Great Inspiration'.

Children keep whistling, make gargling noises,
Just to put their fathers off their metre,
Suddenly they'll shove a frog onto their desks,
Then shout, preventing them from rhyming
Such words as 'frantic'—'romantic', 'winning' and
'running',
'Tractor' and 'tractate', 'insidiously'—'deciduously'.

Every now and then, even in poetry,
There comes an hour for relaxation—
For laziness, short wind, belching, a little yawn—
But this blackout of the spirit doesn't last for ever—
A childish scream will burst out from somewhere,
Piercing the 'peaceful hour', and then explode.

A childish scream is primitively savage,
But only fools and madwomen won't recognize
The greatness of the truth it utters.
Life screams, perched on the carrion it tramples.
A childish scream exasperates you? So it should,
And rightly so: literature does the same!

CHANCE ENCOUNTERS

Chance encounters,
How they're condemned and become
Synonymous with dirt
When dirt itself does the condemning!

And then bogus puritans
Tighten disdainful lips
In fevered alarm
As they frisk their husbands' jackets.

What an explosion of fury
When a hand discovers
A note, an address,
Some evidence of sin!

Accusations of being depraved—
To make you feel like a criminal.
As if you'd been rifling
The sacred family coffer!

Instead, they should remember
That there's nothing more depraved
Than to sleep with your lawful husband
When you don't really love him.

And what is there really
In that not-in-the-least-blind chance,
So totally irretrievable,
Which follows you all the time?

When you're passing, or travelling,
That wild and wonderful chance
Lifts you high above the morass—
Even if it's only for a moment.

In the *Metro* or the suburban train,
In the crowd which has sucked you in,
Amid the welter of facelessness,
Someone's face suddenly surfaces.

And quite without pressure, Life,
Only pressing you at the throat,
Suddenly, irrepressibly,
Throws the two of you together in the crowd.

The future lies hidden in shadows,
But it's simpler to sob out your pain
To someone who's still a stranger
But nevertheless almost your twin.

And better by far than indifference
When you and your wife are in conflict
Is surely a momentary marriage,
Brief, but without feuds and betrayals.

And is such a chance encounter
Really a matter of pure chance,
When its light glimmers in secret
And you dream of it all your life?

And among the sickening cheapness
And boredom with which they are welded,
The accidents of our life
Are perhaps what give it most meaning.

So let them expose you completely,
Smear you and slander you shamelessly—
Remember, without the word 'chance'
The only other word is 'fate'!

LOVE IS ALWAYS IN DANGER

"Love is always in danger"
A Japanese girl said to me,
And all at once the era ground to a halt,
The era of strippers and atomic mushrooms;
And with his trousers half-off, a tourist
Ground to a halt on top of a half-geisha,
And on a sakura a tiny leaf ground to a halt in its growth,
Trembling over the fate of the country.
The youth still half a child froze
As he was rushing to the film 'Sex among Animals',
And so many fingers, bloated, sweaty,
Froze in the act of crinkling *yen*.
Millions of lips froze
A millimetre from a kiss.
On death's naked thighs the equator
Froze like a hula hoop.
The world, right round the globe, is ringed
With one and the same fearful risk.
Chopsticks froze over rice,
And, somewhere, spoons over borshch.

In Cambodia snakes froze and sniffed around
At bombs in the grass,
And, a second before betrayal,
You, wincing, ground to a halt in Moscow.

And I ground to a halt in mid-stride
In the ancient city of Kyoto,
Where, once again, I was looking for someone,
Having forgotten to find myself in myself.
And so, all around, everything *ground to a halt*.
But, just as if their time had now come,
Buddhas stepped down from their pedestals,
Shaking the dust from their rusty hands.

Almost unrecognizable,
They set off in columns
Through markets, bars and restaurants,
Like demonstrators made of bronze.
They walked past the plastic dishes,
Past the beads of the gamblers
And pot-bellied TV's,
The latest Buddha-substitutes.
Through the gilt of weighty foreheads
The Buddhas' wrinkles could be distinguished.
In the Buddhas' hands floated placards:
"Love is always in danger."

The whole world is always in danger
Where wooden shoes step over bones,
Where they even bath children in tubs
Among unexploded mines.
A poet is always in danger
When he lives too safely,
When everything is deceptively clear to him,
And he is not afraid for people.

The globe is strapped on to me.
Like an exhausted Japanese girl,
I carry the whole world around, like a sobbing
Child, on my back.

THE DRUNKEN COW

The cow
        was drinking
                    beer—
Spitting with disgust,
                    but drinking.
One thing was clear to the cow:
Things were going badly for her.
The cow
        drank
            out of fright.
The watchman,
            small, puppet-like,
Forced her mouth open
With a sticky bottle of *Asakhi*.
In the town of Matzudzaka,
Behind the walls of the knacker's yard,
They've a cunning ritual for killing:
Beer,
        massage,
                axe.

Tremble, old man,

      how low can you get!

The cow's destiny is terrible.

She, you realize, is just as Japanese

As you are.

Give her some plain mash,

Give her some plain grass . . .

Let cows, at least,

Be sober in a besotted world!

The cow

   lamented

      sobbing violently,

Swaying like a drunkard.

Her coat was black

Like the black smoke of Hiroshima.

Her groans shook

The gloomy cow temple.

Her seven hundred kilos

Made the earth

     sag.

People are sensitive,

However,

   only

Before the nice warm beef

Has reached the plate.

After the cow had been despatched to paradise

F

We ate by the sweat of our brow,
Grabbing the delicate morsels
Of meat with our chopsticks.
The hostess surveyed the scene proudly.
To this day she remembers
How the actor who played Bond
Praised the *sukiyaki*.
And, sitting at the table,
A drunk with a purple face,
       shouted:
"Friends,
   let's drink
     to the cow,
Who was also a drinker!
For how do we differ from cows
If, simply with a shout of
      'Cheers!'
Somebody pours
Saké and beer down our throats?
Munching hay is a dull way to live.
Our own experience is like the cows'—
Being served before slaughter
A drink and a massage.
And wherever they treat people
Like cattle who drink,
If you don't kick and fight

You're sure to go under.
If a live cow groans,
She's not worth very much.
But after she's been turned into meat,
The price immediately soars.
Let us rise gravely from our mats.
Brothers,
            let's finish drinking in silence
Whatever sister cow
Has left us in our glasses.
In this joyful paradise,
Sodden with the smell of drunkenness,
We even weep beer—
The beer of bleary eyes—
Over the cheapness of our lives,
Over drunkenness in the hour of death,
Over how expensive we are
When they've slaughtered us."

LOVE OF SOLITUDE

In Budapest,
            on Latsi Lajos Street,
Stands a house, dressed in the red armour
                    of autumn leaves.
Not a man,
           or a cat,
               or a dog, whose bark is a comfort,
Lives in it:
           only a woman, living with Russian poetry.
One should raise a monument to this woman during her
                    lifetime
For the way she's translated
               the lowing of the Ryazani herd,
And the howl of Siberian snow storms
              and the literal version of church porches and the
                    block,
Where Russian blood, as yet not washed away,
              cries out in Hungarian.
This is a secret house:
           special, *secret* meetings take place here.

Under the hostess's eyes
                        insomnia shows off its bruises.
Here, Yesenin drinks vodka with her—
                        Tsvetáyeva smokes shag.
Pasternak plays Chopin piano-duets with her.
But unintentionally informing on herself,
Forgetting that ghosts—
                        sooner or later—
                        retreat into the gloom—
"I love being alone!
                I love being alone!"
Defending herself from the night,
                the hostess bangs her fist upon the table.
Oh, dearest lady, what troubles you?
In this cry the soul is stripped naked.
People love solitude out of pain,
Never out of joy!
Solitude brings silence
Which spares us from insult.
Solitude won't hurt you.
Solitude means no offence.
Solitude understands
As a man cannot understand.
Solitude can embrace
As a man cannot embrace.
But the dress is worn on bare
Nerves—
                and all its hooks are red-hot!

"I love being alone!"
                    is to shout
"It doesn't hurt"
                    under torture.
But it *does* hurt,
                    Lord how it hurts,
So that one wishes to hug at least *somebody*.
Solitude: the more it is hated,
The stronger the love.
One should raise a monument
                              to a woman's pain
                                    during her lifetime,
So that she could stand there
                              reproaching men;
                                    stand there for ever.
The refrigerator sighs.
                    It smells of paprika, pepper and *palinka*,
And, going bump down the stairs,
                              apples
                              and pears roll from the loft.
Pain translates from all languages,
                              and from silence.
One should blare out the despised original version
                                    stuck in one's heart:
"I love being alone!
                    I love being alone!"
And then whisper the translation:
                              a defenceless "Don't go!"

WHO WILL GIVE THE ANSWER?

Beside the mine of Chuquicamata
There's a big hill, and on it
Miners, stooping and crushed by their burdens,
Have erected a motto in stone.

They dragged corpses out of the shaft,
The wounded dawn wheezed,
And the motto gleamed over Chile:
'God will give people the answer to everything!'

You, people, admit it, believed
The naive notion of disaster,
Forgetting
            that you erected the motto
Out of worked ore!

Beside the mine of Chuquicamata
Yesterday, (or was it long ago?),
A sub-machine-gun murdered god,
Together with a miner.

And perhaps, in the sky's black mine,
He wheezed through his smashed mouth:
"Why don't you give *me*
The answer to everything?

                     I'll give it to *you*—later!"
But god is always in the miner,
And god is also in you, poet,
The god who, perhaps not soon,
But in the end, *will* give people the answer to everything.

EPISTLE TO NERUDA

Superb,
        like a seasoned lion,
Neruda buys bread in the shop.
He asks for it to be wrapped in paper
And solemnly puts it under his arm:
"Let *someone* at least think
That at *some* time
                I bought a book . . ."
Waving his hand in farewell,
Like a Roman,
            rather dreamily royal,
In the air scented with molluscs,
                  oysters,
                      rice,
He walks with the bread through Valparaiso.
He says:
        "Eugenio, look!
You see—
        over there, among the puddles and garbage,
Landing up under the red lamps,

Stands Bilbao—with the soul
                    of a poet—in bronze.
Bilbao was a tramp and a rebel.
Originally
            they set up the monument, fenced off
By a chain, with due pomp, right in the centre,
Although the poet had lived in the slums.
Then there was some minor overthrow or other,
And the poet was thrown out, beyond the gates.
Sweating,
            they removed
                    the pedestal
To a filthy little red-light district.
And the poet stood,
                as the sailor's adopted brother,
Against a background
                you might call native to him.
Our Bilbao loved cracking jokes.
He would say:
            'On this best of possible planets
There are prostitutes and politutes—
As I'm a poet,
            I prefer the former.' "
And Neruda comments, with a hint of slyness:
"A poet is
        beyond the rise and fall of values.

It's not hard to remove us from the centre,
But the spot where they set us down

                              becomes the centre!"
I remember that noon,
                    Pablo,
As I tune my transistor at night, by the window,
Now,
          when a wicked war with the people of Chile
Brings back the smell of Spain.
Playing about at a new overthrow,
Politutes in Generals' uniforms
Wanted, whichever way they could,
To hustle your poetry out of sight.
But today I see Neruda—
He's always right in the centre

                                  and, not faltering,
He carries his poetry to the people
As simply and calmly

                    as a loaf of bread.
Many poets follow false paths,
But if the poet is with the people to the bitter end,
Like a conscience—

                    then nothing
Can possibly overthrow poetry.

ALDER CATKIN

To J. Butler

Whenever the wind
                    drops an alder catkin into my palm,
Or a cuckoo calls merrily,
                    with trains screaming by,
I fall to reflecting,
                    and struggle to grasp life's meaning,
And, as usual, arrive
                    at the place where it slips from my grasp.
Reducing oneself
                    to a speck of dust in a starry nebula
Is an old way out,
                    but wiser than trumped-up grandeur,
And it's no degradation
                    to realize one's own insignificance,
For in it we realize sadly
                    the implicit grandeur of life.
Alder catkin,
                    weightless as down,
Only blow it away
                    and all changes utterly,

And life, it appears,
                    is not such a trifling matter,
When nothing about it
                    seems merely a trifle.
Alder catkin,
            loftier than any prophecy!
The person who silently
                    pulls it to pieces is changed.
So what, if we can't
                    change the world in a flash, as we'd like—
When *we* change,
                    the world changes too!
We're then transported
                    into a kind of new quality,
As we sail into the distance
                        to a new unknown land,
And we don't even notice
                        the rocking's strange rhythm
On new waters,
            and a completely different ship.
When there suddenly wakes
                    the starless feeling of being a castaway
From those shores
                where you greeted the dawn with such hope,
My dear companion,
                there's no need, take it from me, to despair—

Trust in the unknown
                    alarmingly black anchorage!
What often alarms from afar
                    seems hardly perturbing in close-up.
There too are eyes, voices,
                    the minute glow of cigarettes.
But as you grow used to it,
                    the creak of what seems like a haven
Will murmur to you
                    that no single haven exists.
Translucent the soul
                    which can't be embittered by change!
Forgive the friends who've misunderstood
                    or even betrayed you.
Forgive, understand,
                    even if your lover stops loving you!
Set her free from your palm
                    like an alder catkin.
And don't trust a new haven
                    that starts to enfold you;
Your vocation is
                    the havenless far-off distance.
Break away from the mooring
                    if you become moored by habit,
And cast off again
                    and set sail for a different sorrow.

Let people say:
                "Really, when will he get some sense!"
Don't worry!
                You can't please them all at one time.
What base commonsense:
        "It'll all blow over, it'll all come right in the end . . ."
When it all comes right in the end,
                                there's no point in living.
And what can't be explained
                        is in no way nonsensical.
All reassessments should not worry one in the least—
Since the value of life
                won't be lowered
                                or raised:
The worth of what's beyond value
                        isn't subject to change.
. . . Why am I saying all this?
                        Because one stupid
Chatterbox of a cuckoo
                predicts a long life for me.
Why am I saying all this?
                        Because an alder catkin
Lies in my palm,
                and quivers, as if it was living . . .

VI

SNOW IN TOKYO

Her husband was, it seems, one of those very
Cultured Japanese. That didn't stop him
Slightly despising her because she was,
When all was said and done, a woman.
Every morning he'd sit immersed in books
Bound in thick leather, and whose gilt titles
Were almost rubbed away, and diligently try
To become even more cultured.
She would bring his tea into the library,
And the black lacquered tray which she set down
Had pheasants painted on it,
And on it too lay slices of raw tunny,
Wooden chop sticks,
And a saucer filled with soya sauce.
He would partly notice her, busy as he was
Reflecting on the universal spirit,
And she would go outside to prune the roses.
This she did with heavy silver scissors
Handed down from her samurai grandfather
Who, as well as being a good gardener,

Had been a General, ending his life by *hara-kiri*
After his dust-caked soldier's boots
Had stepped aboard the US cruiser 'Missouri',
And his hands had trembled under the onus
Of the surrender note which had been rustling
In the grasp of his immediate superior.
For quite a while the woman didn't rinse her fingers
Smelling of the garden, and later made a start
On dinner preparations; and while the food was eaten
She'd be presented with the silence of
Her spouse, whose thoughts were of eternity.
Then she would wash the plates,
And a tiny delicate pink petal,
Perched like a butterfly upon her wrist,
Would be washed away, mingling with the water in the
                                                  kitchen sink.
About the same time, the time for meditations
On life and death would terminate, regulated
By her husband's Swiss wrist-watch, and his thoughts,
Having switched off ideas of death, already pointed
Only in life's direction. He'd then slip out
Of his workaday kimono into a clean, crackling shirt,
Breasted with a frost of finest lace,
His wife would help insert into the cuffs
His golden cuff-links showing the rising sun.
Then he would get into his French 'Tergal' suit,

Tapered a little at the waist, tastefully glossy,
And instead of homely *geta* he'd put on
Italian moccasins made from the skins
Of completely innocent Nile crocodiles.
There was no formal leave-taking or
Any indication of when he might return;
His 'goodbye' was the deliberately festive roar
Of the car speeding off into the dusk—
A Toyota van, or, more often, a Jaguar two-seater,
And she'd sit down at the old Chinese mirror
And with her fingertips would try to smooth out
The wrinkles on her forehead, round her eyes
Which, nonetheless, still sparkled youthfully
Like moist dark cherries on the white porcelain
Of her face.
                    The car would return at dawn,
Worn-out like a dog which had run itself to a standstill,
And if its hide had not been polished, thorns
From night-life's thicket would have stuck to it.
Her husband would ask for tea, then Alka-Seltzer,
A great invention of the former enemies
Who'd dropped the A-bomb on Hiroshima,
But also, just the same, suffered from hangovers—
And this drew them close, spiritually, to the drinking
Scions of the Land of the Rising Sun.
Her husband would collapse straight onto the blanket

In his suit, and fall asleep immediately,
And she'd pull off his moccasins—
A flattened cigarette was sticking to one sole,
Its tip, bloodstained with lipstick, she also noted,
As well as a hair from a natural wig from South Korea
Which was now clinging to the 'Tergal',
And also, on the left cuff of his shirt,
One of the rising suns was missing.
Then she would fall asleep;
Following her grandmother's advice, she'd
Conjure up an autumn thicket, and a pond with emerald
                                                    film,
And a blackboard on the still water.
She'd use her gaze to draw, as with chalk, upon the
                                                blackboard,
6.30—the hour of morning awakening,
And, with her gaze, softly sink the board right to the
                                                    bottom,
In such a way, however, that the vital figures shone
From there, through the yellow leaves, rocked by the pond.
One day she was returning from the temple where
Buddha had patiently heard her prayer but hadn't
Given any advice. She suddenly turned her head
Towards the cool columns of the university
Of Vaseda, where she had once studied.
The reason why she turned was partly nostalgia

For her youth, drowned in the still water
Like a leaf filched by the wind from a Sakura tree,
A leaf just yellowing on the branches, just in flight,
But at the kiss forced on it by the slime,
Now drenched completely in the slime's own colour;
And partly because a summoning voice
Was stalking through the columns.
A youth was standing on the steps
Wearing an orange helmet.
This helmet, covered in scars and scratches was
The current headgear of student demonstrators
In Japan, protecting—albeit relatively—their heads
From assault by the police-force rubber truncheons
Which fairly often would rain down upon them.
From underneath the helmet, like a small waterfall,
Seethed some tousled oil-black hair,
And little childish slanting eyes
Glowed, unchildishly embittered,
Opposed in meaning but identical in expression
To the ferocity of warlike samurai
A-brandishing their sabres on the screen.
His hand clasping a microphone, as though it were an apple
From the tree of knowledge, which in politics
Had turned into a new bone of contention,
Convulsively dissatisfied he shouted something
Against the background of a poster with a beard

Resembling Bakunin's, and called for world revolution.
This small and clearly hungry orator was so alone
She felt the urge to feed him, taking from her bag
Delicious dried cuttlefish wrapped in cellophane,
But all the same couldn't quite decide to do it.
And so he went on shouting, waxing furious
At the general apathy of students who rushed shamefully
To the canteen or library, and two of them—
Reactionaries, most likely—started playing
With badminton rackets and a small shuttlecock
Over the helmet of the orator scarred in the global struggle.
And still he kept on shouting, the lone orator,
Shouting out both truths and untruths,
But at least shouting out *something* . . .
And she sensed in that moment
The supremacy of even an impotent shout
Over the slavery of her own dumbness.
Late in the evening, just after the Jaguar
Had glided out of the gates,
She put the children to bed—
And there were three of them: eleven, nine and seven
Very lovely years old, when they don't understand much,
But still, they vaguely guess
At the relations between the grown-ups,
And prefer not to interfere.
And so she put the children to bed

And went out into the autumn night.
This was the birth of the rebellion—
A rebellion without slogans and tanks,
Without any programme, but a rebellion nonetheless,
One of those which flare up imperceptibly
But are not publicized
By the mass-media.

First she went to a café
And started thinking about suicide,
Perhaps because, once,
Akutagava used to sit there
Also thinking about it as he swallowed
Warm saké out of an earthenware cup.
Then the thought passed.
Sadly she reflected on the fact
That suicide was a form of egoism,
And that her children would suffer all their lives,
Also her mother in Nagasaki,
Who bowed to the waist before the Emperor
Staring impressively from a dish hung on the wall,
So that he might pray for her daughter.
And besides, she imagined very vividly
How her husband would order a dress jacket for his
                                                    bereavement,
And, cheerfully posing in front of the pier-glass,

Would hiss at the tailor: "It's tight under the arm",
And ask him to flare the trousers a tiny bit,
As much as would look decent at a funeral.
Damnable life,
Where even dying can't solve anything!

She paid her bill and left.
Then suddenly she saw Tokyo under early snow, unexpected,
Like a hangover hitting you not as you wake up in the

morning,
But before you've plunged into sleep.
Like crumbs of white bread
Aimlessly revolving in a fish-tank,
The snowflakes swirled whitening the backs of passing cars,
And even the autumn dirt under the twentieth century's

feet.
She laughed, like a worn-out geisha
Who suddenly feels that she is unemployed.
A geisha's free only to be cold and hungry,
But the joy of a rebellion of the soul
Lies in bringing as little as possible of the so-called useful
To our so-called society.
She caught the light white flakes of freedom
And licked them from her palm, before they melted.
Accompanied by the snow she wandered
Right through the night along the Tokyo streets,

And the snow showed her many districts
She'd never visited before. The snow led her
By the hand towards an entertainment-booth
Where a woman in a ragged golden leotard,
Wriggling just like a snake, ate a *real* snake,
Sinking her wide-gapped crooked teeth,
Which lived a separate life, one from another,
Into the body of the snake whose head,
Torn off only a moment earlier was lying,
Incidentally, on the wooden rostrum,
With its beady eyes still quite alive,
While living quivering bits of body
Convulsed inside the gullet
Of the unfortunate snake-swallower.
Damnable life,
In which you swallow sorrows like bits of snake,
While life
Imperceptibly swallows you also, bit by bit.

The woman hurried out of the entertaiment-booth,
Tucked herself up in the snow's wet snout,
And it led her into the distance, as if it were a dog
Waving its dirty white tail.
Then she began to feel cold. Her coat
Was far too light,
Her flimsy lacquered shoes

With their blunt cut-out toes
Cheeped, like ducklings,
Gulping the dirt with the snow
Through their black open beaks. By a marble fountain
Still gushing out water, foolish against the snow,
She sat down on a soaking bench,
On somebody's decomposing newspapers
Which had portraits of the leaders of the ruling party,
And also leaders of the opposition,
And fell asleep at once; and clumsily the snow
Tried to protect her from itself,
Wrapping her all up from head to toe
Inside a blanket sometimes gentle and fluffy,
But sometimes meltingly wet.
She awoke from somebody's gaze.
Someone unknown was standing there before her
Wearing an unfashionable hat with large spots
On its shiny worn ribbon.
In a hand densely covered with grey,
He held a tattered umbrella which covered his head.
He was in jeans unseemly for his years,
And all over them—this was the strange thing!—
Happy flecks of paint seemed to be leaping
Like a rainbow in the midst of a snow storm.
"Come with me. . ." said the unknown man
And took her freezing hand;

Then they dived into a basement,
Stepping over the rats which poked about on the stairs,
And, thrusting his umbrella somewhere into the murk,
With the words: "This umbrella is my key",
The unknown man
Either opened the door, or something resembling a door,
And they entered what looked like a house.
The host didn't switch on the overhead light,
But only a strange standard lamp,
On whose coloured shade, once it was plugged in,
Tints, which then came to life, began writhing enigmatically.
The host placed a coffee-pot on the electric stove
And gave her some hot coffee in a plastic mug.
He didn't ask about anything.
Out of the lumber he produced a shepherd's simple reed pipe,
Just like the one she had seen
In her childhood at Hokkaido
In the hands of a drunken barefoot peasant,
As he led cows doomed from birth to the slaughterhouse,
And tried to bring a little colour to their
Last steps on the grass.
The host drew from the pipe the pure trembling sounds
Of a half-forgotten folk song,
And began a shuffling dance around his guest,
Seated on an old stool cracked by the heat,
And she, having removed her shoes, was pointing her feet

In sodden stockings in the blissful direction
Of the electric stove. The host's eyes were those
Of one who, while knowing nothing about her,
Had known her even in childhood, had known her in youth,
Had delivered her children,
And had helped her to pull off her husband's moccasins,
And had sat somewhere close to her in the café,
Having noticed her suicidal thoughts
Drifting in a light cloudlet of smoke
Above the tiny cup of coffee in her hand.
But he, playing on the reed pipe,
Expressed no condescending pity,
But with a whirling turn of melody
And his sad but smiling eyes,
He said to his guest:
"All passes away—
Of course, life too will pass away—that can't be helped!
But if we *are* alive, why die before our time?
We're all of us doomed, like cows from birth,
But there's also the joy of playing a reed pipe
Or listening to one played by someone else.
And very likely there are in each of us
Some notes which seem impossible to reach,
But all one needs to do is quietly close one's eyes,
Stretch out expectant hands, palms upward,
And suddenly there appears in them, as if

By magic, the wooden body of a pipe,
And all one needs to do is press one's lips
To the round holes bored into this mystery,
And mingling with our breath there flows from us
Our only melody—
Then life will never pass away
But death *will* pass away, having glutted its ears with life."
And the guest, hearing these words
Uttered only by his eyes,
And by his lightly dancing reed pipe,
Started not exactly to cry, but to liberate herself with tears,
Giving birth to tears like thousands of little children,
And, without being aware of it, she fell asleep
On the aluminium camp-bed,
Wrapped up in a soldier's old greatcoat,
Which smelled of peace, not war.

When she awoke,
First of all she saw pictures.
Pictures hung on the walls, stood, or simply lay around.
They were quite different from the pictures
She used to choose with her husband
When buying decorations for the house
In the Ginza galleries.
The pictures there had resembled extensions to furniture.
The pictures in Ginza—a lavish luxury-market—

Didn't make conversation, didn't shout,
But only mildly massaged the mood
Like masseurs whose tongues had been cut out.
But these pictures shouted, conversed,
And even sang songs on a reed pipe;
And if they were silent, then even the silence
Resembled a shout or a whisper.
But dominating all these pictures was War;
Not the parade-ground, bemedalled war of Generals,
But the filthy, bloody, typhoid-ridden war of soldiers,
War not pretending to be grand!
She was struck by one picture in particular:
The artist had called it 'Rebellion'.
It showed the well-tended hands of someone or something
invisible,
With shirt-cuffs, on one of which,
She seemed to notice,
One rising sun remained,
And next to it the other had fallen out
And lay neglected in the dust.
The well-tended hands presented a soldier with a small
medal
Manufactured from atomic mushroom cloud.
The soldier, swollen and frightful to behold,
Like a drowned man with a dead face the colour of khaki,
And eyes like swamps,

Pointed his rifle butt, covered in blood still moist,
Towards that bit of metal, the image of the fallen cuff-link,
In a gesture of scornful rage and eternal rejection.

The guest looked around, hoping to find the artist,
But he had evaporated and it seemed as if
All these pictures had in fact painted themselves.
Only on the home-made trestle
Which served the host as bed and table
Lay a note:
"I won't be back before evening. Make yourself at home",
And beside it there rocked, as if living,
As if moulded out of yesterday's snow, two eggs.
She cracked them very carefully,
As if afraid to cause them pain,
Made scrambled eggs, boiled coffee,
Then taking a brush from its repose
And dipping it into the paint, started
Moving it across an untouched canvas,
And this was like liberating herself with tears,
Except that the tears now had a different colour.
Of course, she had learned painting while at school,
Or rather had copied from things, not painted—
Like an apple, perhaps, or a jug.
But now she yearned for something different:
To copy from what was inside her,

And to copy from what was not—
From the air which smelled of the reed pipe.
Something was being born, through the paint's tears:
And this was her face,
And this was not *her* face,
But the face that lay within:
The face behind the face.

She left that basement
Before her host returned,
Took a taxi and went home
Through the town which had foolishly trampled
The snow which fell to earth as foolishly.
Her husband rushed at her in fury.
She—
Made a sign in his direction,
Not one of scornful rage,
But irrefutably rejecting him, like reality,
Which, if you think about it,
Is only real if you submit to it,
And her husband turned tail, terrified, feeling
That here was a different woman, whom he did not know.
She went towards the nursery, kissed
Three small dark heads smelling of soap and sleep,
And, asked where she had vanished to for so long,
Replied:

"I was listening to a reed pipe in a field."
Next morning
She drove the Toyota van to a shop
And carried home a multitude of paints:

Cadmium-lilac, yellow, purple,
Light red and dark red;
Ochres—muffled and golden,
Brown Mars, orange Mars,
Whites: lead, zinc, titanic,
Greens: emerald green, bright 'Paolo Veronese' green;
And browns: 'Van Dyke', natural umber,
Archangel brown,
Bluish-brown 'caput mortuum',
Blacks: peach black,
Burnt Ivory,
Grape black
(Actually, as it happens, made from grape pips),
And also ultramarine,
Berlin azure and Turkish blue;
Oils: nut oil and linseed oil,
Varnishes: mastic and pistacchio;
Brushes: bristle, squirrel, badger, Siberian mink,
As well as palette knives and spatulas
Of various sizes and pliancies,
Coloured pencils, stylographs,

Easels, sketching-pads, under-frames,
Canvasses, primed and unprimed,
Paper in rolls, sheets of Whatman,
And also hammers and pliers,
And nails both large and small
For every purpose, except for one: hammering
Into her fellow humans' palms.

Now the rebellion was becoming armed.

Quite calmly she demanded of her husband
That he should clear the flowers immediately
Out of the Winter greenhouse.
On hearing this he shook his head slightly,
But quite alarmed gave in to the request
Made by his wife, now quite out of her mind!
This was the first building taken in the rebellion.
And then she started painting, and would admit
Only children to the rebellion's headquarters,
And, at first, only her own.
And they, dazzled by such a quantity
Of pencils and clean paper, switched themselves on
To the rebellion's wavelength,
And, filled with cheerful malice, depicted
Father resembling an octopus,
As well as an octopus resembling father.

She did not favour that direct approach
In her attack upon the 'status quo',
But delegated it to her civic-minded children.
She combatted ugliness not by direct *exposé*
But by the essential beauty of mixing colours—
For the strongest opponent of ugliness
Is the human spirit, stripped to its purest form,
And not basely-framed indignation
At the supremacy of baseness.

She painted cows she remembered from Hokkaido
With the oppressed eyes of the women of Japan.
She painted the women of Japan
With the oppressed eyes of the Hokkaido cows.
Her husband took her away to Africa, hoping this way
To dissipate her sudden urge.
They travelled luxury class
And even had a license to shoot elephants.
But the jungle didn't in the least attract her
With its toilets punctuating every path.
What really appealed to her was the tumbledown huts
Made of palm leaves and bamboo
Where women, using wooden pestles,
Pounded batatas into flour;
And so she painted African women
With the oppressed eyes of the women of Japan,

And she painted the women of Japan
With the oppressed eyes of African women.

And one day *Experts* visited the converted greenhouse:
Not the kind that does the rounds at private shows
So as to hold, in one hand, a daiquiri in a frosted glass,
And, with the other, free, or rather *ostensibly* free,
Hand, to wave majestically
To the talents of this world,
And obsequiously, following the mighty of this world,
Not even guessing that they're wrong in their assessments,
Since the world's main motive force
Is talent, and not force itself.

The two Japanese experts who arrived at the greenhouse
Were two old men *in no way* of this world,
But envoys from the great world of the great Hokusai,
Rublev, Bosch, El Greco,
Even talking of Pablo Picasso
As being competent, but frivolous nonetheless.
There was something childlike about these two old men,
And perhaps this was the reason why
The not-so-young woman, but very young artist,
Let them enter the studio where
Before only children had been admitted.

The first old man, despite the heat,
Wore a severe black suit, and round his neck
Wrinkled by passage of governments,
A garish Parisian foulard,
Given to him in the '20's in Montparnasse
By a girl-friend he had snatched
From Eluard, who was only just beginning.

The second old man, whose mouth showed specimens
Of prime Krupp steel produced even before
Hitler came on the scene, (unfortunately, even then
It didn't lose its quality), appeared in tennis shorts,
Holding a Dunlop racket, but all the same
He wore a pair of simple *geta*.

The artist was very frightened that the Experts
Wouldn't confer on her the rank of artist.
And feeling a failure, she hardly looked at them
While shifting canvasses around, just like a cart-horse,
And asking: "Is it catching the light too much d'you think?"

The first old man asked her: "Have you been painting
                                                    long?"

He had a stony, other-worldly look.
She hurriedly answered: "Yes."
The second old man asked her, without concern:

"Have you exhibited before?"
And she dejectedly admitted "No."
"Who taught you?" asked the first.
"A man," she answered edgily.
"Ah ha . . ." and he took back his tactless question.
The second, tapping for some reason, with his racket
Against the frame of the picture under inspection,
As if testing its solidity,
Remarked with an unexpected smile:
"I think *this* one's rather more like it . . ."
"Like what, like whom?" she uttered, twitching nervously.
"Like painting . . ." he smiled faintly;
The first, a little piqued at not having got in first,
Added: "I feel the same about it
As my distinguished colleague,
But I don't advise you to hurry to exhibit."
The second, twirling his racket on the floor,
Said, and here he giggled slyly,
"And I *do* advise you to hurry,
Although there is a grain of sense
In what my colleague said.
Of course, one loses by hurrying too much,
But one gains nothing by not hurrying at all.
To conceal works of art from the people
Is just the same as robbing them.
But if a person who conceals them is

Not just anybody, but the artist himself,
Then it is, forgive me, nothing but egoism.
And, by the way, don't you have a glass
So that I and my colleague might join you
In a toast to your first exhibition?
My colleague and I will undertake
All the arrangements, isn't that right, colleague?"
"Of course, of course . . ." mumbled the other,
"When I advised you not to hurry,
I was advising like a father,
But sometimes childish wisdom is superior
To the wise unhurriedness of fathers . . ."

Oh, how great is every artist's need
To be *called* an artist,
Not by ignorant illiterates,
And not by empty-headed groupies,
Wetting themselves in ecstasy,
But by two old men who have gorged themselves on paint,—
By imperturbable *Experts!*

And so three glasses placed in the middle
Of the perkily rocking racket,
Right in the very middle,
A bit discoloured by play,
Decided the whole thing, and the exhibition took place.

It took place, alas, in Ginza,
For which the artist felt no love at all,
And, by one of fate's little ironies,
In that new giant department store
Where her husband used to buy his braces,
Cuff-links, neckties and other personal trifles.
He too, incidentally, came on the opening day,
And in spite of being so immensely cultured,
Secretly felt no pride at all,
But a wild, almost animal, feeling of terror:
His wife was finally slipping beyond his reach.
The department store building became
The second one taken during the rebellion,
Although, unfortunately, not completely.

An old man wearing colourful jeans went up to her,
And she knew him at once, not by his jeans,
But by his strong grey hands
In which a reed pipe danced invisibly.
Her first word to him was "Teacher . . ."
But he waved it away with a gentle gesture,
Saying: "Teacher? In art, I don't know what that means.
'Teacher'—that word's an empty kind of medal,
Even if one receives it from the kindest hand.
In art, what can be more unnatural
Than so-called relationships

Between so-called teachers
And their so-called pupils!
We're both artists, and so we're friends and enemies,
And our tender hostility will help protect
Each of us, but mutual reverence will destroy us.
I can respect you as a forceful enemy,
And if things ever should go wrong for you,
Remember, find your way to that old basement—
That's where you'll find a cup of coffee,
And I'll gladly play to you again on the reed pipe . . ."
The exhibition had one rather strange feature:
While men, of course, dropped in to see it,
The women literally flocked there, as to a shop
Where they handed out freedom from husbands and the
                                                daily grind,
And even women from the embassies—
White women all the way from Europe
And also some from the United States,
Stood there for hours examining the canvasses,
Recognizing their own sufferings painted
In the eyes of Japanese and African women
And of the doomed cows from Hokkaido,
And seeing in the turbulence of rebellious colours
Their own repressed desire for rebellion.
One enterprising manufacturer
Placed in the miscellaneous leather goods

Department of this selfsame store
Thousands of leather handbags,
With white characters on a black background
Spelling out a short but eloquent "No".
And after visiting the exhibition,
And walking down only a single floor,
Women would acquire these handbags
Bearing the slogan of moral rebellion
Against men—the disparaging "No".

One day the artist had a visitor;
It was a Japanese woman in her early forties,
Wearing a cheap kimono, not made of silk;
Her eyes were the oppressed eyes of the Hokkaido cows,
In which, however, there clearly glimmered
The bonfires at the outbreak of rebellion.
"I'm from the Sony factory," she said, "of course
I'm nothing like as educated as you,
I've never done a painting in my life,
But now, I beg you, teach me how to paint!"
The artist started giving her lessons,
And something came to light in that woman
Who, in her watercolours, would depict
Other Japanese women assembling transistors—
Dustbins for the world's lies and music.
These factory women seemed to resemble

Lotuses buckling under the burden
Of heavy snow, but the woman painting
Them stood straighter with each successive painting.
Then the woman from the Sony factory
Brought a friend with her—a box-office attendant
From the Kabuki theatre, and *she*, in turn,
Brought *her* friend—an actress from a rival
Theatre, and *she* brought a friend—
A boxer's wife, whose husband sometimes
Used her face for sparring practice.

In a short time the greenhouse witnessed the birth
Of a kind of underground organization,
Struggling, if not to procure men's downfall,
Then at least for something like democracy.
Certain women only stayed a certain time,
Coquettishly wishing to intimidate
Their husbands with art, which they then deserted
For doubtful peace within the family's bosom.
But other women stayed very much longer
And formed some sort of executive committee.
And, as in most committees, there were plots and intrigues,
Which soon had no connection with the purity
Of the original idea. And the artist sometimes
Would regret that she had got mixed up
In all this business, where art quite unavoidably

Had started smelling of politics—extremist politics
At that! Women's liberation from men?
That kind of programme was one-sided:
For men, as well, are far from being free,
Let's say, at least, in their own jobs, from bosses.
And often, though it's dreadful to admit,
In their own homes, from domineering wives.
The mutual liberation of men and women—
That was the programme she accepted;
And, having in mind this noble, ultimate aim,
Perhaps for ever unattainable,
And for this reason still more noble,
She hadn't the heart to close the fragile doors
Of the revolutionary headquarters,
(That is, the greenhouse), in the faces
Of new legions of aspiring women.
The greenhouse was shaken by contradictions,
Since people's championing their individual styles
Was deemed by their opponents as betrayal
Of the revolution's ideology.
Here one could find little realists,
Little surrealists, little abstractionists,
Pop artists, as well as op artists,
And each of these directions made the claim
That it alone was worthy of first place.
The artist tried to reconcile them all,

Using the principle of the carrot and the stick.
But all the same they'd scratch each other's pictures
With their palette-knives, and use the turps,
Reserved for final touches to their *chefs d'oeuvre,*
For splashing, irreconcilably, each other's faces.
Besides, despite their stated hatred for the male sex,
When any man appeared inside the greenhouse,
Quite unobtrusively, they'd preen themselves
Ready to bite out each other's throats.
But, nonetheless, with all these listed drawbacks,
This was indeed a rebellion,
And which rebellion
Ever got going without victims and other losses?
And the artist, worn out in the struggle,
Continued, not only painting pictures,
But also heading the rebellion
Which it was now impossible to abandon;
For deprived of wisdom in its leadership
It could turn into a rebellion against its own.

And the artist steadfastly headed the rebellion,
Conscious that she had also made mistakes,
But convinced at the same time of her own rightness,
And that of the rebellion, as such,

For life is a rebellion against death,
And art is a rebellion against life
If life and death become too much alike.

. . . But sometimes, if snow appeared outside the window,
The artist felt an urge to go out into it
Away from all the meetings and the votes.
And, filled with relief, she would remember
That somewhere out there was a dingy basement,
And living in that basement was an artist,
And in his strong grey hands, a healing reed pipe.

(Tokyo—Moscow)